The Love of the World Cured
By Nathaniel Vincent

I0220874

The Love of the World Cured
By Nathaniel Vincent

Edited and updated by C. Matthew McMahon and Therese B. McMahon
Transcribed by Blake Gentry

Copyright © 2012 by Puritan Publications and A Puritan's Mind

Some language and grammar has been updated from the original manuscript. Any change in wording or punctuation has not changed the intent or meaning of the original author(s), and has been made to aid the modern reader.

Published by Puritan Publications
A Ministry of A Puritan's Mind
4101 Coral Tree Circle #214
Coconut Creek, FL 33073
www.puritanshop.com
www.apuritansmind.com
www.puritanpublications.com

This Print Edition, 2012
Electronic Edition, 2012
Manufactured in the United States of America.

ISBN: 978-1-938721-49-6
eISBN: 978-1-938721-48-9

CONTENTS OF THE TREATISE

MEET NATHANIEL VINCENT

[Vincent's Portrait by John White (1681) from the National Portrait Gallery]

Nathaniel Vincent (1639?-1697), nonconformist puritan divine, was probably born in Cornwall about 1639 (*cf. epist. Dedication* to *A Present for such as have been Sick*).

His father, John Vincent (1591-1646), son and heir of Thomas Vincent of Northill, Cornwall, born in 1591, matriculated from New College, Oxford, on Dec. 15, 1609, became a student at Lincoln's Inn in 1612, and, afterwards taking orders, was beneficed in Cornwall. Of nonconformist leanings, he was driven there by his bishop, as well as from so many other livings that it was said no two of his seven children were born in the same county. Coming to London in 1642, he was nominated by the committee of the Westminster assembly to the rich rectory of Sedgefield, Durham, but died after holding it but two years, in 1646. His widow, Sarah Vincent, petitioned on Nov. 1, 1656 and in April 1657 for 60£ which her husband had lent to the parliament (Cal. *State Papers*, Dom. 1656, pp. 146, 147, 185, 191, 329; Addit. MS. 15671, cf. ff. 38, 42, 55, 69, 114, 124, 140, 148, 150, 219, 227, 238, 251). Their eldest son, John, who inherited his grandfather's estate of Northill, is confused by Mr. Wood with a son of Augustine Vincent (*Athenæ Oxon.* vol. i. p. xxxv). The second son, Thomas, is separately noticed.

Nathaniel, the third son, entered Oxford University as a chorister on Oct. 18, 1648, at age 10. He matriculated from Corpus Christi College on March 28, 1655, graduated with a B.A. from Christ Church on March 13, 1655-6, M. A.

on June 11, 1657, and was chosen chaplain of Corpus Christi College. He was appointed by Cromwell one of the first fellows of Durham University, but never lived there. At twenty he was preaching at Pulborough, Sussex, and at twenty-one was ordained and presented to the rectory of Langley Marish, Buckinghamshire. There he was ejected on St. Bartholomew's day, 1662, after which he lived three years as chaplain to Sir Henry and Lady Blount at Tittenhanger, Hertfordshire. About 1666 Vincent went to London. There his preaching at once attracted attention, and a meeting-house was shortly built for him in Farthing Alley, Southwark, where he gathered a large congregation. In spite of fines and rough handling by soldiers sent to drag him from his pulpit, he continued boldly preaching during the stormy times. In July 1670, soon after his marriage, he was confined in the Marshalsea prison. He was removed to the Gatehouse, Westminster, on Aug. 22 (*cf.* Cal. State Papers, Dom., Addenda, 1660-70, p. 546). He remained six months in prison. In 1682 he was again arrested, brought before magistrates at Dorking, and sentenced to three years' imprisonment, after which he was to be banished from the country. A flaw, however, was perceived in the indictment, and, after the section expenditure of 200l., Vincent was released, but so weakened from illness that he was long unable to preach (Letter to his Congregation, 24

June 1683). He was again arrested in February 1686, this time on an improbable charge of being concerned in Monmouth's rebellion (Wood, Life and Times, ed. Clark, iii. 179). Some of his books were written in prison; thus "his pen was going when his tongue could not."

Vincent died suddenly on June 22, 1697, in the fifty-ninth year of his age. He was buried at Bunhill Fields; (see *Inscriptions on Tombs in Bunhill* Fields, 1717, p. 34). His funeral sermon was preached by Nathaniel Taylor.

Wood's *encomium* on Vincent is unusually high, "He was of smarter, more brisk, and florid parts than most of his dull and sluggish fraternity can reasonably pretend to; of a facetious and jolly humour, and a considerable scholar."

The *works* of Nathaniel Vincent are as follows:

1. *The Doctrine of Conversion*, or, *The Conversion of a Sinner Explained and Applied*, London, 1669, 8vo; with which is published 2. *The Day of Grace* (same date). 3. *A Covert from the Storm*, London, 1671, 8vo (written in prison). 4. *The Spirit of Prayer*, London, 1674, 8vo; republished, 1677, 8vo; 5th edit. 1699; other edits. Saffron Walden, ed. J. H. Hopkins, 1815, London, 1825. 5. *A Heaven or Hell upon Earth*, London, 1676,

8vo. 6. *The Little Child's Catechism*, whereunto is added several Short Histories, 1681, 12mo. 7. *The True Touchstone*, London, 1681, 8vo. 8. *The More Excellent Way*, London, 1684. 9. *A Warning given to secure Sinners*, London, 1688, 8vo. 10. *The Principles of the Doctrine of Christ: a Catechism*, London, 1691, 8vo. 11. *A Present for such as have been Sick* (sermons preached after his recovery from sickness), London, 1693. 12. *The Cure of Distractions in attending upon God*. 13. *The Love of the World cured*. 14. *Worthy Walking*. The dates of the last three do not appear. Sermons by Vincent are in Annesley's *Continuation of Morning Exercises*, London, 1683, and in his *Casuistical Morning Exercises*, London, 1690; reprinted in vols. iv., v., and vi. of Nichols's edition, London, 1814-5, 8vo. Vincent was much in request for preaching funeral sermons; five or six were printed in quarto. He edited the *Morning Exercise against Popery* (London, 1675, 4to), twenty- five sermons preached in his pulpit at Southwark by eminent divines.

For further study:

Clark's *Indexes*, vol. ii. pt. i. p. 280, pt. ii. p. 308; Foster's Alumni (1500-1714); Neal's Puritans, iii. 521; Calamy's Continuation, i. 30; *Alumni Westmon.* p. 129; Burrows's *Visitation*, pp. 171, 173, 369, 477; Bloxam's *Reg. of Magd. Coll.* v. 208; Palmer's *Nonconf. Mem.* i. 304; Wood's *Athenae Oxon.* iv. 617; Wilson's *Hist. of Diss. Churches*, iv. 304 (this is the most accurate account); Cal. *State Papers*, Dom. Add. 1660-70 pp. 273, 388, 464, 1671 p. 556; Taylor's Funeral Sermon, 1697, 4to; Wood's *Life and Times* (Oxford Hist. Soc.), ii. 561; *Hist. MSS. Comm.* 11th *Rep. App.* p. 46; *Notes and Queries*, 2nd ser. ix. 267.

Taken in part from the National Dictionary of Biography, public domain.

[ORIGINAL TITLE PAGE]

THE

LOVE

OF THE

WORLD

CURED.

In several sermons preached on
1 John 2:15, "Love not the world."

To which is added,
A sermon preached some while ago on James 4:3, "Ye ask, and
receive not, because ye ask amiss, that ye may consume it
upon your lusts."

By
Nathaniel Vincent, M.A. Minister of the Gospel

"From the least of them even unto the greatest of them,
everyone is given to covetousness," (Jeremiah 6:13).

LONDON,

Printed for *Brabazon Aylmer*, at the *Three Pigeons* over against the
Royal Exchange in *Cornhill*, 1696.

INTRODUCTORY LETTER

To the citizens of this famous city of London, particularly those worthy people who desired the publication of these sermons.

Great dangers, if they are not apprehended, become much greater and more difficult and unlikely to be avoided. Many men will confess that sin is evil, and that Satan is an enemy, who yet are not persuaded that the world is so perilous an adversary, as the Holy Scripture speaks about it; where indeed, to be delivered from this present evil world, is a part of that salvation in which Christ is the Author, as well as to be rescued from the prince of darkness and redeemed from all iniquity. There is a war between heaven and hell. Evil angels are endeavoring to make men rebel against the God of heaven, that those who are naturally bad may become worse and worse, and more despise his commands and authority, who is most rightfully the Lord of all.

Now earth joins with hell in this war. And earthly things are the great weapons which the powers of hell make use of to carry it on. Edged tools are to be meddled with, not without great wariness and caution. Worldly things are this way; how many minds have they divided with care! How many consciences have they wounded! How many souls have they defiled, and made utterly unfit, both for the service of God and for his kingdom!

You that are citizens and traders have great dealings in the world, and you have need to guard both heart and tongue, eyes, hands, and feet; for all are in danger by the mammon of unrighteousness. Remember that you have to do with an enemy and deceiver, which has cheated thousands of their souls, and of an eternal inheritance. Let your souls be so wise as to commit themselves every day into the hands of the Father of Spirits, that they may be preserved unspotted from the world, and kept in your duty, which is well-doing.

You are only stewards of what you get in the world, and must be called to an account of what you have done with it. What you obtain by unjust and wicked ways is not likely to be well, but wickedly used; and the account will be rendered with grief and horror, when it shall be found that you have really stolen a great part of your estates, by defrauding and over-reaching your brothers, and by this have done the greatest wrong to yourselves. Let no blot cleave to your hands. Take clean steps wherever you go. He that works righteousness and walks uprightly, walks surely, and shows the truest wisdom. Take heed of incurring the curse of the Lord that is in the house of the wicked. Value the blessing which is on the habitation of the just.

If you are enriched with righteousness, truth, and mercy, if you behave holily, justly, and blamelessly with whoever you deal with, by this means a blessing will be on what you have, what you leave, and who you leave it to, if they walk in your steps. Let those Scriptures be written on the fleshly tables of your hearts, and ever recurring to your remembrance. Lay up for yourselves a treasure in heaven, where neither moth nor rust corrupt, and where thieves do not break in and steal. And riches do not profit in the day of wrath, but righteousness delivers from death. The gain of the whole world will profit no man if his soul is lost forever.

In a battle, soldiers take care to be well armed. This world is really fighting against you, as well as the God of it. Have on the shield of faith in Christ, the breastplate of love to God, the helmet of hope of a better world hereafter; these weapons will be found mighty and effectual for your safety, and will gain your victory.

While you are in the world, there are plagues of several sorts, that are very infectious, and that spread in all places; and the very best churches are not out of danger of the contagion. It concerns you to never be without an antidote. And if this one prescript of the Great Physician of souls, "Love not the world," but be minded and followed, the world that passes away, being undervalued, will be less able to infect and hurt you, and yourselves will be better able to do the will of God, that you may abide forever.

As for you, my dear and much respected friends, *who being affected with the hearing of these following words, yourselves, hoped the publishing of this treatise might have some* good effect on others. May it be according to your desires and hopes! And may you all be wise merchants, heavenly traders, and truly wealthy, with durable riches and righteousness!

I conclude this address to you in the inhabitants of London, and its suburbs, with this wish, that you may have so much of the world as is best for you! That you may love it no more than it deserves! That you may do much good with it! That you may be blessed with more enduring good things than those of the world are! And that you may be fellow-citizens with all the saints of the best of all cities, which has eternal foundations, whose Builder and Maker is God!

Your faithful monitor, and humble servant for Jesus' sake,
Nathaniel Vincent

THE LOVE OF THE WORLD CURED

"Love not the world," 1 John 2:15.

This chapter begins with a strict caution against sin. Sin is the worst evil on earth, and hell itself cannot show a greater evil. But as bad as this evil is, there is a remedy to be found against it in the Gospel; and this remedy is *sufficient* and *effectual*. Jesus Christ, whom the Gospel reveals, is the propitiation for the sins of the whole world; and all that believe in him, whatever their offenses have been, have him, who is the Righteous One, the Maker of their peace, and their prevailing Advocate with the Father. Such believers abide in him; they walk as he walks; and they especially yield obedience to that great command of *love*.

The apostle was very apprehensive of the danger that believers are in from Satan, who draws the most of men to sin, and by sin, to ruin. And he signifies that if the Word of God abides in them, they would by this become strong enough to withstand and overcome the wicked one.

And having so cautioned them against sin and Satan, he admonishes them of their peril from this present world; which is very apt to bewitch and ensnare the hearts of men, to attract and draw their affections, which it is utterly unworthy to have bestowed on it. Now to wean and keep hearts loose from the world, is that which the apostle designs; therefore with great plainness and authority, he gives this charge in the text, "Love not the world;" for this love and the love of God are inconsistent, and cannot be in the same heart together. Everyone that has an ear should hear what the Spirit speaks to the churches against the love of the world. But alas, how few will hearken to it! Lord, who will indeed believe that this is really your command, "Love not the world!" Men's love naturally runs downward, towards the earth and earthly things, with a strong and violent current. How mighty and miraculous that grace must be; which makes the heart to flee from the world, and to be driven back from the pursuit of it; and causes the stream of the affection to run upward, toward those things which are above!

At the hearing of this text, "Love not the world;" many may be ready to cry out, as the disciples did when they were told, how hard it is for a rich man to enter into the kingdom of heaven. "Who then can be saved?" And truly since the love of the world is so common in the church itself, it is a plain demonstration that salvation is not so common a thing as is commonly imagined. Certainly few will be saved, few will enter into life, and into that everlasting kingdom that is above; for few mind it, or strive to enter into it; and unto this entrance, and unto the salvation of vast multitudes, love of the world is the grand obstruction and hindrance.

In the text, there are two observable *particulars:*

1. Here is a great *idol,* and that is the *world.*

2. Here is the *worship* that is forbidden to be given to this idol, and that is *love.*

1. Here is a great idol, and that is the world. It is the idol of thousands and millions, even of the greatest part of mankind; and there is just ground to fear that it is the idol of the greatest part of the visible church of Christ. Where pagan and Romish idolatry is down, this idol, the world, keeps up in the hearts of men, that they are without number. The sun, the moon, the hosts of heaven, though they have been so very much idolized, yet nothing compares near as much, nor by so many, as this world and the things of it.

2. Here is the worship, that is forbidden to be given to this idol, and that is love. Our Lord tells us that love is the first and greatest command. The highest degree of our love is the highest and most acceptable worship, which God requires to be given to himself. Now to see this love misplaced on the world, which is so vain, so evil, it must necessarily provoke him to jealousy.

The **DOCTRINE** which I raise from the words is this: *The love of none should be set on this present world.* What should be is one thing, what is, is generally quite completely the contrary. The world conjures and keeps the hearts of most alive, within its own circle; but it is their fault and folly to be so confined. There are three things which are to be denied to the world; our faith, our hope, and our love. Our trust should not be placed in it, we should expect no great matter from it, and by no means should we cast away our love on it. By faith the world should be overcome; our hope should be of things unseen; and our love should be raised far above all things here below. "If ye then be risen with Christ; seek those things which are above, where He sits at the right hand of God; set your affection on things above, not on things that are on earth," (Colossians 3:1-2).

In the handling of this doctrine, I *shall*:

First, give you a description of the world, and a kind of map of it, out of the Word of God.

Secondly, show you what that love of the world is, which is forbidden.

Thirdly, demonstrate how unreasonable it is that the world should have the love of any set on it.

Fourthly, make application.

In the first place, I am to describe the world to you, that you may better understand it; and with it understand how little reason you have to be in love with it.

THE WORLD

1. The world, though at first was created very good, by sin entering into it, has lost its glory. Man, who was made to have dominion over the creatures, was at first made upright, and while he kept his first estate; and continued in his primitive righteousness and integrity, there was a beauty and order in this lower creation. There was nothing at all amiss or defective in the Creator's workmanship. When God had finished the work of creation, and reviewed the whole, "he saw everything that he had made, and behold it was very good; and the evening and the morning was the sixth day," (Genesis 1:31).

But sin did sad work when it came into the world! How it marred and sullied what the Lord had made excellent. The apostle tells us that the creatures are a great means to bring us to the knowledge of God, whose creatures they are, "For the invisible things of him from the creation of the world, are clearly seen, being understood by the things that are made, even his eternal power and Godhead," (Romans 1:20). But how apt are the creatures to confine the minds of men; and while they busy themselves so much about these, the Creator is not minded, his Godhead is neglected, his power is condemned. We read, "The heavens declare the glory of God, and the firmament sheweth his handywork," (Psalm 19:1). But sin has made the luminaries of heaven to be admired and worshipped, and so the God "that above has been denied," (Job 31:28). In this lies the beauty of the world, that God was visible and seen to be glorious, in the whole frame and parts of it; but that beauty, as to fallen man, is gone; the creature, instead of declaring the glory of God to man, rather obscures and hides it from his eyes; instead of leading the heart up to him, it rather leads the heart of man away from him. Therefore, natural men are said to be ἄθεοι ἐν τῷ κόσμῳ, "without God in the world," (Ephesians 2:12). The world interposes between God and them, and alienates and estranges their minds from him.

2. The world is a dark place. "We have also a more sure word of prophesy, whereunto ye do well that ye give heed as unto a light that shines in a dark place, until the day dawns, and the daystar arise in your hearts," (2 Peter 1:19). All nations of the earth, until visited with the dayspring from on high, have a dark veil of ignorance on them. We read, "Of the face of a covering cast over all people, and a veil spread over all nations," (Isaiah 25:7). The world deserves to be called, not only the region of darkness, but of the shadow of death too; to show how deadly and destructive their ignorance will prove, if they live and die in it. The apostle speaks of the darkness of this world, of which evil and apostate powers are the rulers.

How the prince of darkness works in the dark, even what he pleases!

In this dark place, how few see God, or have the sense of awe of him on their spirits! "Beloved, follow not that which is evil but that which is good; he that doeth good is of God; he that doeth evil hath not seen God," (2 John 1:11). How few understand the things which belong to their peace! Jerusalem itself is wept over by our Lord, being in the dark as to these matters: "If thou hadst known even thou at least in this day the things that belong to thy peace! But now they are hid from thine eyes," (Luke 19:42). In this dark place, how few find the narrow path, or see to the end of the broad way! "Enter ye at the strait gate; for wide is the gate, and broad is the way, that leadeth to destruction; and many there be that go in thereat; because strait is the gate and narrow is the way that leadeth unto life, and few there be that find it," (Matthew 7:13-14). The Lord compasses the paths of men, and is acquainted with all their ways. Death is just before them, and hell follows with it; time is drawing to an end, and then comes eternity; yet most are so much in the dark, that none of this is perceived. They go on in the dark, and in the unfruitful works of darkness, and do not know what they are doing, nor where they are going. "The way of the wicked is as darkness, they know not at what they stumble," (Proverbs 4:19); and at length they fall into destruction, and the blackness of darkness forever.

3. The world is subject to vanity, and so becomes a vexation of spirit. "The creature was made subject to vanity not willingly, but by reason of him who hath subjected the same," (Romans 8:20). The whole creation, groaning and travailing in pain together, may cry out, "Fye on man," for this subjection to vanity. That wise and wealthy king of Israel, Solomon, who had so much of the world that he could not desire more; extracted the utmost which was found in it; and what he found in it, he himself informs us, "Vanity of vanities saith the preacher, vanity of vanities, all is vanity," (Ecclesiastes 1:2). He that had all worldly things in the height, says they are vanity in the height; and not so much as one thing that this world can show, is to be excepted.

This vain world raises hope high, and then frustrates it; and this is a matter of great vexation. Great matters are expected from the world, while at a distance, and before we come to possess it; strange kinds of felicity and contentment are imagined in it, except that which we have in our eye and hope is attained to the enjoyment of it. Alas, *pro thesauro carbones (coals for the treasure)*; we find it to fall many many degrees short of what we fancied. This vain world vexes the men of it; for it seems to be of some substance, but really is not. "Wilt thou set thine eyes on that which is not? For riches take to themselves wings and fly away as an eagle towards heaven," (Proverbs 23:5). This world is trusted in for security, but it is found only to be a castle in the air; and instead of shielding, rather exposes to danger. "The rich man's wealth is his strong city, and an high wall in his own conceit," (Proverbs 18:11). He conceits it to be so, but it may vex every vein of his heart, when by sad experience, he finds it to be no such matter.

4. The world is under a curse. As soon as men fell into sin, he fell under the curse; and the ground itself was cursed for man's sake, "Cursed is the ground for thy sake, in sorrow shalt thou eat of it all the days of thy life," (Genesis 3:17). And not only the element of earth, but air, and fire, and water, are all cursed to the children of men for sin's sake; how much harm do they inflict by these! The curse is on all men in their natural state; "Cursed is everyone that continueth not in all the things which are written in the book of the law to do them," (Galatians 3:10). And natural men, being cursed and polluted, all things that they have are cursed and impure to them; "To them that are defiled and unbelieving is nothing pure," (Titus 1:15); and what is impure cannot be blessed to them.

Behold, how the curse cleaves to and follows the disobedient, and mixes itself with whatever they enjoy; "Curse shalt thou be in the city, and curse shalt thou be in the field; cursed shall be thy basket and thy store; cursed shall be the fruit of thy body, and the fruit of thy land, the increase of thy kine, and the flocks of thy sheep; cursed shalt thou be when thou comest in, and cursed shalt thou be when thou goest out. The Lord shall send on thee cursing and vexation and rebuke in all that thou settest thy hand to do until thou be destroyed, and perish quickly; because of the wickedness of thy doings by which thou hast forsaken Me," (Deuteronomy 28:16-19).

The things of the world are given to wicked and worldly-minded men in anger, they take occasion by it to abound in sin; for their lusts have them, and what they have at their command; and on this divine displeasure, and their own woe is increased. To go with a curse at the last day into everlasting fire, will be terrible; and truly at present it is very sad to go with a curse to one's trade, to one's house, to one's business, to one's bed, to one's table. It is very dreadful to have that Scripture take hold of anyone. "Let their table be made a snare, and a trap, and a stumbling block, and a recompense to them," (Romans 11:9).

5. The world is that which the evil one is the god of; so Satan is called, "In whom the God of this world hath blinded the minds of them that believe not, lest the light of the glorious gospel of Jesus Christ should shine into them," (2 Corinthians 4:4). Although Satan spoke too boldly and

peremptorily, and falsely too, in speaking universally to our Lord Jesus, "All this power will I give thee, and the glory of them; for that is delivered unto me, and to whomsoever I will give it," (Luke 4:6), yet there may be something of truth in what he says; for if all had been utterly false, and Satan could have given nothing of what he offered, where was the force and strength of his temptation? It must indeed be acknowledged that the Lord's kingdom rules over all. And that Satan's power is limited; but yet through divine permission the things of the world may be at Satan's disposal. As he stripped holy Job naked of the good things he had, all of a sudden; so if he has leave from above, he may furnish the wicked with plenty and abundance.

He may gratify the ambitious with worldly greatness, the covetous with gain, the voluptuous with sensual delights. As Satan put it into the heart of Judas to betray Christ, so he took care that the thirty pieces of silver were brought to him, to make him turn indeed as a traitor.

The world being thus in the hands of the devil, and he being the prince of it, (John 12:31); the world becomes more dangerous to the children of men. He can set it off with great advantage, that it may be more alluring and enticing. Satan, with great subtlety, applies himself to the various tempers and humors and inclinations of men. How he magnifies preferment and applause, and earthly grandeur to the proud!

How he paints forth the pleasures of sense to those who are so brutish to admire them! What gratifies the ear, the touch, the taste shall not want a most extravagant commending, as if these lower pleasures were a perfect paradise. And if he has to do with those that are lovers of worldly wealth, how he makes silver and gold to glisten in their eyes! This god of the world is not lacking to put a varnish on the things of the world, that he may delude and deceive those whose hearts are inconsiderate and foolish and naturally prone to deceive themselves.

It should debase the world in the thoughts of all to consider that it is Satan's great engine by which he keeps up his kingdom, and carries on his destructive designs against the souls of men. Here I need to warn you with great caution. How bad is it to have what you have out of the devil's hand (ἐχθρῶν ἀδῶρα δῶρα). As the kisses, so the gifts of enemies are deceitful; whatever Satan may pretend, he does not intend real kindness to any, but ruin.

6. The world is the pitiful portion which fools choose. That man very well deserved to be called a fool, who minded nothing but the filling of his barns and belly, and making provision for this present life, "But God said to him, Thou fool, this night thy soul shall be required of thee, and when whose shall those things be which thou hast provided? So is he that layeth up treasure for himself, and is not rich towards God," (Luke 12:20-21). Holy David was wise in desiring that his soul

might be delivered from the hand of the wicked, and from being of like mind, who minded only a "portion in this life," (Psalm 17:13-14). They must be forever; their portion can be enjoyed, and last only for a moment. Therefore, they must necessarily be forever destitute and poor and miserable. Our Lord denounces a woe to the rich, for "they have received their consolation," (Luke 6:24). Their consolation itself is sorry, and quickly ends; and then their endless woe begins.

If a man had a pearl in his possession that was worth thousands; and like Cleopatra, dissolved it, and drank it down at one draught, and left himself nothing to live on, this would be a piece of folly that all would blame. If one born to, and in possession of a great estate, should fall and waste it all in one week's riot; and become and live as a beggar for many years after; everyone would censure such gross inconsiderateness. But this is only small foolishness to that of the worldly-minded, who regard only their living, as they count well, for a few years, but are utterly ignorant regardless of what becomes of them forever. That man must necessarily be granted void of understanding; who, though he must of necessity exist to eternity, yet minds only those things that are temporal.

7. The world is of a polluting and defiling nature. We read of the *pollutions of the world*, "For if after they have escaped the pollutions of the world through the knowledge of the Lord and Savior Jesus Christ, they are again entangled therein,

and overcome; the later end is worse with them than the beginning." The things of the world deserve to be called *irritamenta malorum*, the great irritations and provocations to evil; how much wickedness they are the occasion of! There is much evil in a vehement inclination, and resolution to get the world, "They that will be rich, fall into temptation and a snare and into many foolish and hurtful lusts, which drown men in destruction and perdition," (1 Timothy 6:9). He that peremptorily resolves if he possibly can, to be a man of estate, what wickedness is there that he will not venture on, that he may obtain what he designs? Neither their fear of hell, nor hope of heaven shall hinder him in what he is pursuing after.

There is dealing with sin in the providential "keeping" of the world, when God calls to distribute and communicate; but an uncharitable heart makes a close fist; and though all has been received from God, yet little or nothing is given forth for his sake. And how do men load themselves with sin, when they resolve to secure the world and hold it fast, though it stands in competition with Christ, and they make shipwreck of faith and of a good conscience! There is a sin also in the using of the world, because it is so apt to be abused; provision being made hereby for the flesh to fulfill its lusts. The apostle plainly intimates that those who have dealings in the world are very prone to be entangled in the affairs of it, and to be spotted and defiled by it. Therefore he tells us, that "pure religion and undefiled before God and the Father is this, to keep ourselves unspotted from the world," (James 1:27).

8. The world is a great enemy to Christ and souls. It makes men enemies to the cross of Christ. "For many walk of whom I have told you often, and now tell you weeping, that they are enemies to the cross of Christ; whose end is destruction, whose God is their bellies, whose glory is their shame, and who mind earthly things," (Philippians 3:18-19). Those who mind earthly things are most unwilling to take up the cross and follow Christ; and they will not comply with the design of Christ in his crucifixion. His design was to reduce and bring back to God the fallen sons of men, who had apostatized and departed from him; "For Christ also suffered once for sins, the just for the unjust, that he might bring us to God." Now that we may be received by him, we must come out from the world. "Wherefore come out from among them and be ye separate saith the Lord, and touch not the unclean thing, and I will receive you, and will be a Father to you, and ye shall be my sons and daughters saith the Lord," (2 Corinthians 6:17-18)

The young man in the Gospel turned his back on Christ, and slighted treasure in heaven; because his great possessions had his greatest love, and the highest place in his heart. This enemy, mammon; how many does it hinder from coming to the Lord Jesus at the call of the Gospel, and when they have begun to come, how many has it drawn back from following him! The world being thus an enemy to the Savior of souls; and hindering the acceptance of salvation; must necessarily be an enemy to souls themselves. Millions of souls have been lost, that this world might be gained.

9. The world is the very suburb of hell itself. It is a place far off from heaven, and bordering on destruction. The men of the world are continually on the bottomless pit's brink, and are in perpetual danger of falling into it. The world is Satan's walk, (Job 1:7). When the Lord said to Satan, "From whence comest thou?" He answered, "From going to and fro in the earth, and from walking up and down in it." The apostle signifies the same, "Be sober-minded, be vigilant, because your adversary the devil walketh about like a roaring lion, seeking whom he may devour," (1 Peter 5:8). And how many become his prey! Here it is that the vessels of wrath are fitted for destruction; by filling up the measure of their iniquities.

The world is indeed the saint's slaughterhouse, though it is not worthy of them. The faithful worthies here spoken of, "had trial of cruel mockings and scourgings, yea moreover of bonds and imprisonments; they were stoned, they were sawn asunder, were tempted, were slain with the sword; they wandered about in sheep skins and goat skins, being destitute, afflicted, tormented; of whom the world was not worthy; they wandered in deserts and in mountains, in dens and caves of the earth," (Hebrews 11:36-38). And wicked men who are the fondled darlings of the world, are by this more exposed to Satan, and furthered in the broad road which leads to perdition. They are stupid and senseless and spiritually dead while they live in the world; and within a short time they are chased out of the world, though loathe to depart; and are seized by temporal and eternal death together.

10. The world is that which thousands are continually going out of, and the fashion of it passes away. The days in this world which a man has to live, are only a few, "Man that is born of a woman is of few days and full of trouble," (Job 14:1). "Man dwells in an house of clay whose foundation is in the dust, and is crushed before the moth. They are destroyed from morning to evening, they perish forever without any regarding it," (Job 4:19-20). All perish forever so as to be cut off from the world, without hopes of ever returning to it again; though most perish forever too in another sense, being punished with the destruction that is eternal; yet few lay this to heart.

Death is continually sweeping away the inhabitants of this world with the power of destruction. In all the four parts of the world, perhaps not above four or five or a few more, are to be found alive; that were born a hundred years ago. Among the ancient Romans, they had some games that were called *Ludi Seculares*, secular games; which were celebrated some say every three hundred, some every hundred and ten; others once in a hundred years. And before the celebration of them, it used to be cried: *Venite ad ludos quos nemo mortalium vidit, neque visurus est. Come to those games which no mortal man alive ever saw, or will see again.* Every hundred years, how the world is emptied of the former; and new dwellers come in their room. Here is no continuing city; no, the world itself will shortly be consumed, "But the heavens and the earth which are now by the same word are in store, reserved unto fire, against the day of judgment, and perdition of ungodly men," (2 Peter 3:7). And since there is no continuing city here, what serious seeking should there be of one that is to come, (Hebrews 13:14). Even that city that has firm and everlasting foundations whose builder and maker is God! (Hebrews 11:10).

In these particulars I have given you, *Veram & accuratam totius orbis terrarium tabulam, a true and accurate map of the whole world.* You may see what is in it; you may look to the end of it. It is full of vanity and trouble, and lies in wickedness. All that love it are blinded and deceived by it; and must quickly leave what they love; and then they will be forced to acknowledge that in choosing the world, they made a very ill choice, and that this charge, "Love not the world," was needful.

WHAT IS THE LOVE OF THE WORLD?

In the second place, I am to show you what the love of the world is, which is forbidden in the text. This is necessary, because the love of the world is usually called by extenuating names; and many will plead for it, though never so sinful, as if it were their wisdom, and in some respects their duty to harbor it.

1. Love of the world is forbidden which blinds and perverts the judgment. It is an observation which has a great deal of truth in it in diverse regards, *Omne perit judicium, cum res transit in affectum. Vehement affection bribes the judgment to give a wrong dictate and determination.* You find such a perverted judgment, "This their way is their folly, yet their posterity approve their sayings," (Psalm 49:13). The heaping up of wealth and endeavoring to perpetuate their names, they judged to be their greatest wisdom; and though this was their folly, yet those that followed after were of the same mind.

Likewise, "Whilst he lived he blessed his soul, and men will praise thee when thou doest well to thyself," (Psalm 49:18). The judgment of the worldly and wealthy man is so blinded, that he thinks his soul to be blessed, and himself to be most happy, when his heaps of riches are greatest; and foolish and injudicious ones are ready to applaud him, as if getting much of the world were doing most good to one's self.

Love of the world most wickedly prevails, when it turns the light that is in us into darkness; so that we are not able to discern anything better than these worldly enjoyments: when it turns the mind to an infidel; the other world is looked on with a strange eye and is counted a matter of derision, rather than desire; and little credit is given to that supernatural and most certain revelation: Christ our "Savior has appeared," and has "abolished death, and has brought life and immortality to light by the Gospel," (2 Timothy 1:10). This present world cannot but be disparaged by the revelation of a better world; if it is indeed believed. Now love to this world is indeed strong, when it banishes faith; and the Gospel itself shall be questioned, and denied by many, that earthly things may more eagerly and delightfully be pursued.

2. Love of the world is forbidden, which stupefies the conscience, so that it exercises no authority, nor causes any restraint; and whatever is done, as long as it is gainful, conscience has no remorse at all. Coveting after the wealth and pleasures of the world will stupefy the conscience almost as soon as any sin whatsoever. The language of the epicurean, "Soul take thine ease, eat, drink, and be merry, thou hast goods laid up for many years," (Luke 12:19) plainly manifested

that doting on his great estate and carnal delights, had cast his conscience into a dead, and indeed, deadly sleep.

How many go up and down, saying, "Who will show us any good?" And they conclude the good things of the world to be the best, and are the only things which they inquire after; and in this diligent inquiry, conscience does not give them the least check, nor does it chide them for their being so much taken with lying vanities. Neither does it upbraid them for their neglect of God, of Christ, their soul, their duty, and of a lasting treasure in heaven. What a monopoly the world has gotten of the hearts and affections of such men! Certainly the world is very high, no, has the highest place in their hearts, since it has gripped their consciences under its feet!

3. Love of the world is forbidden, which overcharges the heart with care about it. Our Lord gives a caution against this care: "Take heed least at any time your hearts be overcharged with surfeiting and drunkenness, and the cares of this life, and so that day come on you unawares," (Luke 21:34). These cares *overburden* and *depress* the souls of men, so that they sink into this earth; and all their solicitousness is about earthly things, how they may be obtained and secured. They stick fast in the thick clay with which they load themselves and look no farther. It is very ill when care and trouble about many things causes a carelessness, and neglect of the one

thing that is needful; and Martha is looked on as a wiser woman than Mary.

This overcharging care is altogether needless, for the Lord himself cares for those who cast their cares on him; "Casting all your care on him, for he cares for you," (1 Peter 5:7). He gives us leave, no, requires us, to ease ourselves of the whole burden of our cares, by casting it on him; and his care, how significant, securing, and beneficial it will be found to be! And as this overcharging care is needless, so it is hurtful, for it is a great hindrance to our truest and most real profit and advantage. This care makes the word unprofitable, and the hearers of it unfruitful, or if some fruit is brought forth, it is indeed from ripening so, as to be acceptable; "And that which fell among thorns, are they, which when they have heard the word go forth, and are choked with cares and riches and pleasures of this life, and bring forth no fruit to perfection." So much care and concernedness about the world shows the heart's love to it, and that it is too much taken with it.

4. Love of the world is forbidden, which makes it to be desired and chosen rather than the grace of God, and glory in the world to come. Lovers of the world do not mind what the grace of God has appeared to teach them. "For the grace of God which bringeth salvation hath appeared to all men, teaching us that denying ungodliness, and worldly lusts we should live soberly, righteously and godly in this present

world," (Titus 2:11-12). Though we live in the world, worldly lusts are to be denied; we must deny to harbor them, we must deny to fulfill and gratify them; but these worldly desires and inclinations wholly sway the world's lovers; they condemn the benefits of Christ, washing, sanctification, justification in his name, and by his Spirit; and a treasure in heaven, though so safe and lasting is a poor thing with them, in comparison of an earthly treasure, though "moth and rust can corrupt it, and thieves can break through and steal it away," (Matthew 6:19-20).

Love of the world rules in the hearts of men, when things that are sensible and visible, as most suitable and vest for them; are made choice of. Communion with God and his Son Christ Jesus, the riches of his grace, are looked on as mere talk and fancy by those whom the love of the world has befooled. Worldly comforts and enjoyments are preferred and esteemed as having the most solid and substantial goodness in them.

So while a worldly heart holds fast scales, vanities are over-valued as if they were for worth the weightiest things.

An excellent man in his poetical fragments, speaks this to our present *purpose:*

> *When flesh was weighing thou put'st in*
> *Thy love and the eternal crown,*
> *Against a feather and a sin; down.*

And yet it thought, these weighed Thee

It had been wiser to have thought,

The earth is weighed down by a fly,

Than to prefer a thing of nought

Before the love of God most high.

But all worldlings are senseless and sottish. That was the language of One born from above, "Whom have I in heaven but Thee, and there is none on earth, that I desire besides Thee," (Psalm 73:25). The language of the lover of the world is quite contrary, "What is there in heaven that I count worth my minding! And there is nothing on earth but earthly things, which I desire; and many days, that I may have a long enjoyment of them!"

5. Love of the world is forbidden, which causes the greatest fear, lest the world should be lost, and the greatest grief at the loss of it. It was truly said by the poet, *Res est solliciti plena timoris Amor. Love is full of solicitous fears about the beloved object*, lest anything should happen that may deprive or hinder the enjoyment of it. Lovers of the world are much more afraid of losing their *earthly* substance, than they are of losing their *immortal souls*. Though our Lord says, the gain of the whole world is unprofitable, and cannot make up the loss of one soul; (Matthew 16:26). They, for their parts, are of another

mind, as if one world was of more worth than all the souls that are in it.

Fear of losing what they love makes them safely lock up their earthly treasure! How do they fear a bond that is no security! How afraid they are of a false title to an estate! But evil spirits and fleshly lusts that war against their souls; they do not fear, nor guard against; and as to their well-being in another world, they are not at all concerned; or anything, though never so insignificant, satisfies them.

And as love raises the greatest fear in the worldling, lest it should be taken from him; so when it is lost, especially if a great deal is lost together, what a spring tide of overwhelming grief and sorrow comes! The apostle speaks of sorrow of the world, and tells us that it works death, (2 Corinthians 7:10). The world is, as it were, the soul of a worldling; if that takes wing, and flies away from him, no wonder that his heart is ready to die away within him. Millions of sins did not cost him a tear, though he has committed thousands of millions, his spirit was never contrite and broken. But the loss of a few hundred or thousands of pounds breaks his heart. He weeps and mourns, and will not be comforted because they are not. Love to the world makes him say, at the loss of it, "I do well to be angry, discontented, and sorrowful even unto death."

6. Love of the world is forbidden, which fills the heart with the greatest joy, because the good things of the world are possessed. That prohibition, "Thus saith the Lord, Let not the wise man glory in his wisdom, neither let the mighty man glory in his might; let not the rich man glory in his riches," (Jeremiah 9:23) plainly shows what men are naturally inclined to boast of as a matter of their solace and joy; when worldly wisdom and might brings in worldly wealth, and secures the possession of it; this makes the worldling's heart glad above all, for he has no greater joy than to have his worldly possessions prosper. We read of the triumphs and joy of the wicked, such as it is, and it is short, the ground of it is slippery, the foundation is next to nothing, "Knowest thou not this of old since man was placed on the earth, that the triumphing of the wicked is short, and the joy of the hypocrite but for a moment," (Job 20:4-5). The reason of this joy is growing great and high in the world, "his excellency mounts up to the heavens, and his head reacheth unto the clouds," (Job 20:6).

These lovers of the world "trust in wealth, and boast themselves in the multitude of their riches," (Psalm 49:6). Riches are gloried in, because they think that they may depend on them, both for security and contentment, though they often find themselves disappointed; and then their joy is turned into sorrow. If having the world causes the greatest joy, certainly love of the world is idolatrous. Job was judged to be a hypocrite by his unkind, censorious friends; but he demonstrates by many arguments that he is sincere, that he "had not made gold his hope," nor said to the "fine gold, thou art my confidence;" that he had "not rejoiced because his wealth was great, and because his hands had gotten much," (Job 31:24-25).

Those that have, should be as though they possessed nothing; and therefore they should joy as if they received nothing. I read, "Delight thyself in the Lord and he shall give thee the desires of thy heart," (Psalm 37:4); but it is a truth, "Delight thyself in the world, and thy desires never shall be satisfied."

7. Love of the world is forbidden, which commands the time and labor, so that the greatest bent and endeavors are in pursuing after it. The psalmist tells us, "'tis vain to rise up early, to sit up late, to eat the bread of sorrows," (Psalm 127:2), but though it is vain, yet this is the worldling's practice. The beloved world makes him go to his bed late, and quickly raises him up from it again; his strength is wasted in going up and down at mammon's bidding, and laboring in mammon's service; and his pains are not grudged, no, he concludes that they are well bestowed, though all this while he is wearying himself for every vanity.

Love makes men mad on this idol, the world; they talk, they act as if they were besides themselves. You would conclude a man to be frantic, if you saw him eagerly running in the streets after bubbles and feathers; the things of the world are no better, which worldlings busy themselves so much to obtain. What the apostle speaks concerning his love to Christ; is applicable to their love to the world. Whether they are besides themselves, it is to the world; or whether they seem to act more soberly and with consideration and judgment, it is for the world's sake; for the love of the world constrains them to live to the world, though at death the world will not at all avail them.

8. Love of the world is forbidden; which is continually increasing without any fear of danger. They certainly love the world too much, that think they can never love it enough. Indeed, love to God can never be excessive; when it is highest, it falls infinitely short of that which he is worthy of; it is infinitely below what his perfections claim as due to him. But love of the world may easily exceed due bounds, and be a great deal more than so poor a thing deserves; and when it is immoderate, it is a wicked love, and an occasion of much wickedness. It is a true observation,

Crescit amor nummi quantum ipsa pecunia crescit. As wealth abounds, so it is more abundantly loved. The psalmist's caution is needful, "If riches increase, set not your heart on them,"

(Psalm 62:10); which means by intimation, that the more there is of the world, the more the heart is apt to be drawn away after it.

He that lays the reins on the neck of his affections, and suffers them to run out after the world without check or restraint, the more he loves the world, he still desires more of it, and is further off from satisfaction. "He that loves silver shall not be satisfied with silver, nor he that loves abundance, with increase," (Ecclesiastes 5:10). Abundance makes him more craving, and no increase will content him. And while he enlarges his desire as hell, what haste he makes towards hell! As worldly love increases, so will the Lord's jealousy; and how hot and consuming will that jealousy be found! Those stupid souls who imagine they can never love or have too much of earthly things, go the way to deprive themselves of all: "Woe to them that join house to house, that lay field to field, till there be no place; that they may be placed alone in the midst of the earth. In mine ears said the Lord of Hosts, of a truth many houses shall be desolate, even great and fair without inhabitation," (Isaiah 5:8-9).

9. Love of the world is forbidden, which makes all cautions and counsels against it to be derided, and the lusts of it are securely notwithstanding all, fulfilled. Such kinds of lovers and servants of the world were the Pharisees; their pretenses were high and specious as to the service of God, but

mammon was in their aim, their affections; and on this they bestowed their heartiest labor. When our Lord said, "No servant can serve two masters; for either he will hate the one and love the other, or else he will hold to the one and despise the other. Ye cannot serve God and mammon," (Luke 16:13- 14). It follows, "the Pharisees also which were covetous, heard all these things, and they derided him."

The worldling, instead of trembling to hear that covetousness is idolatry, will be a strong and effectual bar to admission into the heavenly kingdom, "No covetous man who is an idolater, hath any inheritance in the kingdom of Christ and of God," (Ephesians 5:5). I say instead of trembling at this, he inwardly smiles and laughs in his sleeve; and he secretly resolves that no sermons or discourses shall beat him off from prizing and pursuing a thing of so much worth, as worldly wealth in his judgment is. Whatever preachers say in the pulpit, they shall never persuade him to undervalue that which is dearer to him than his very soul, he can give the hearing to all that they say; and the bare hearing is all that he gives, for his heart "goes after his covetousness still," (Ezekiel 33:31). And the lusts of the flesh shall still be gratified with sensual delights, the lusts of the eyes with earthly treasure, and the pride of life with the honors of the world. *Hac tria pro trino Numine Mundus habet. The world has these three gods.* The truth is, the worldling has the *world* for his deity; and in this, his trinity, is pleasure, wealth, and honor.

10. Love of the world is forbidden, which looks at martyrdom as madness, and death as misery; because the world and worldlings are by this parted. Those hearers compared to stony ground, had too much love to the world, to suffer or part with anything for the word of Christ. "Yet hath he not root in himself," (Matthew 13:21), the world was too fast rooted in him, "but endures only for a while, for when tribulation or persecution arises because of the world, by and by he is offended." Lovers of the world cannot do away with the yoke of active obedience; commands are too strict for them; but the burden of the cross is counted intolerable. They think it strange concerning the fiery trial that any should abide by it. They would rather venture on hellfire, than that at a stake.

They do not have faith to believe, that the "sufferings of this present time, are not worthy to be compared with the glory that shall be revealed," (Romans 8:18). Neither does it have any influence on them when they are told, that their light afflictions which are but a moment, work for suffering saints a far more exceeding and "eternal weight of glory," (2 Corinthians 4:17). They are all for securing the possession of present things; hopes of future, their foolish hearts think are vain; and they deem it wisdom, rather to make shipwreck of faith and a good conscience, than to cast the beloved world overboard.

But though they avoid sufferings from men by carnal shifts, these lovers of the world are at last seized on by death, and then they are forced to leave their all behind them. O! miserable worldlings who die three deaths in one! There is a separation between the soul and God; and they and the world are parted to eternity. Body and soul will have an ill and sad meeting again at the last day; but their place on earth will know them no more, and they will be forever banished from the Lord's presence. When dying perhaps, death most afflicts them because it chases them out of the world; but when they are sent to their long, doleful, and eternal home; they will perceive that the beloved world befooled them too late, all the while they were in it, and has quite left them in endless misery.

How Unreasonable it is that People Should Love the World

In the third place, I am to demonstrate how unreasonable it is, that the world should have the love of any set on it. I shall prove evidently, that the worldling so misplacing his affections on earthly things, acts as one not only void of grace, but void of reason.

1. Love of the world is inconsistent with an interest in the Father's love. I find this argument in the verse where my text lies, "If any man love the world, the love of the Father is not in him." And life itself is but a trifle, is compared with this love of God. "Thy lovingkindness," says the psalmist, "is better than life," (Psalm 63:3). In another place he cries out as one under a sweet astonishment, "How excellent is thy loving-kindness O God!" (Psalm 36:7). How excellent it is, no tongue can utter, no heart can comprehend. This love may well be called the fountain of life; the life of grace is from it, which the people of God are blessed with. "I will call them my people which were not my people, and her beloved which was not beloved," (Romans 9:25), and the gift of this love is "eternal life through Christ Jesus our Lord," (Romans 6:23). No, to this love of God, that gift of gifts, Christ himself is owing. "Herein is "Love, not that we loved God, but that he loved us; and sent his Son to be the propitiation for our sins," (1 John 4:10).

None that have this love can be miserable, none can be happy without it, whatever they have besides. This love of God makes friends to be profitable and friends indeed; it can make enemies to be at peace with us; and all things to be ours; ours, to be subservient to our truest welfare. Any of those who are interested in this love, will find it permanent and constant, unchangeable in life, unchangeable at death; and after death it will endure forever. Of the Lord it may truly be said, to everlasting he is God, and to everlasting he is love.

But the lovers of the world keep themselves effectually out of God's favor; they were born strangers to him, and children of wrath; and love of the world fixes them in their estrangement from God, and fastens the wrath of God on them. The Lord of heaven and earth never stands neuter to any man; that is to say neither friend nor foe to him. If he is not the one, he is certainly the other. He hates all whom he does not love, and is a terrible enemy to everyone who is not reconciled to him through a Mediator. Now the worldling values the world so highly, that the favor of God is nothing in comparison to him, and all his other sins have provoked divine displeasure and indignation against him. So his flight from God's love; makes the anger of God to be the hotter and fiercer against him; and his hatred of him the greater. And how can the worldling's heart endure, or his hands be strong, when God that hates him, shall deal with him in a way of wrath and vengeance! (Ezekiel 22:14).

2. The love of the world is inconsistent with the grace of love to God. To the whole dirty tribe of these men who so greedily mind and covet the things of the world; those words are rightly applicable, "I know that ye have not the love of God in you," (John 5:42). Though God is so excellent in

himself that he is worthy to be the admiration and desire of men and angels; though he has been so patient and kind to these unthankful worldlings themselves; though there is no good thing that they have, but is of this great benefactors bestowing, yet they do not love him; they take no notice of his hand out of which comes all that they receive, but both himself and all his goodness is despised. "Or despise thou the riches of his goodness, and forbearance, and longsuffering, not knowing that the goodness of God leadeth thee to repentance?" (Romans 2:4). If unexpected good comes to these lovers of the world, they are so blind themselves, as to attribute it to blind chance and luck; which ought to be ascribed to divine providence, which strives to overcome their evil with goodness. Or, if their own care, contrivance, and endeavors have been successful, God is not owned in that success; they will not take notice of any obligation they are under to him; but they bless themselves in themselves, and in their own craftiness, for doing well to themselves. Thus they of old did "Sacrifice to their own net, and burnt incense to their own drag; because by them their portion was fat and their mean plenteous," (Habakkuk 1:16). Worldlings will look anywhere but upward, where they should look chiefly. Their hearts are alienated from God through the blindness that is in them, and love of the world has blinded them.

Now how wretched are those hearts which are wholly destitute of love to God! All the duties they perform to him, without this grace of love, become mockery, sin and abomination; because they disobey the great command which requires that God should be loved with all the heart and soul and strength; no other command can be rightly kept, nor obedience be accepted. Those that do not love God are unfit to enjoy him, and how may they tremble to think of appearing at his tribunal, who neither love him, nor are beloved of him!

3. Love of the world is wronging of the soul of man. What is spoken concerning the hatred of wisdom, may be applied to the love of the world. The world may truly say, "Whosoever covets me wrongs his own soul, all that love me love death." The world having insinuated itself, and gotten mastery over, and possession of the affections; makes the soul to forget itself, and its immortal nature, and its vast capacity; by which it is capable of far higher, better, and more durable blessedness than a poor short-lived earthly felicity. The worldling's soul has lost the use of right reason, and sense and fancy guide and govern his reason instead; he discourses nothing of a saint, and little of a man; but how much of the brute, in his appetite and inclination! Man that is in honor, and abounds in wealth, and understands nothing better, is "like the beasts that perish," (Psalm 49:20). The psalmist, when under a temptation, was envious at the foolish,

admiring the prosperity of the wicked; for he saw that they prospered in the world and increased in riches. But as soon as he came to himself, he cries out "so foolish was I and ignorant, I was as a beast before thee," (Psalm 73:22), intimating that a soul, which can never die, is never more infatuated, than when it is taken with the lying and dying vanities of this world.

A lover of the world is a cruel man to his own soul, he never minds what his soul ails, though it is sick of many deadly maladies; he does not provide the suitable food for it, nor proper clothing; he is not concerned at the danger his soul is in, because it is in the hands of a destroyer and a murderer; neither does he regard where his soul must go, as soon as it leaves its earthly tabernacle.

The worldling's soul may cry out on him, and justly reproach him after his manner. O you foolish in the worst sense and bloody man. You mind me no more than if you were a mere brute, and had not the soul and understanding of a man in you. Your body is pampered and fed to the full, but I your soul am quite empty; your body is clothed and adorned, but I am stark naked. You are heaping up worldly wealth, but to make me your soul rich towards God you have no regard; and the saving of me which is the great salvation, you neglect. O cruel man! You are false to me, to yourself; and do not consult your truest interest; for me your soul, you have no care of; but sottishly and securely you suffer me to be sinful, miserable, starved and lost, and damned to eternity.

4. Love of the world is very opposite to religion and godliness, in the power of it. Covetousness is often times covered with a form of godliness, but it causes the power of godliness to be denied, (2 Timothy 3:5). This power of godliness lies in a rectified judgment; which discerns the excellency of spiritual things; and in the steady bent and inclination of a sanctified heart towards God and true goodness; this power of godliness, is in a sense a kingly power. "For the kingdom of God is not in word but in power; it rules and commands the whole man," (1 Corinthians 4:20); it restrains from the minding of vanity, and from the working of iniquity; and it constrains to the doing of duty, and working out our own salvation. It constrains to the following after God for himself, as the surest Guide, and as the best portion that can be enjoyed.

But where love of the world is in power, how can the power of godliness be, or be exerted? If any think to divide their hearts between God and the world, they are void of understanding and sincerity; "Their heart is divided, now shall they be found faulty," (Hosea 10:2). This parting of the love, though seemingly into equal shares, between God and the world; argues a true love to the world, but none to God; for he is not truly loved at all, unless he is loved above all things.

Love of the world eats out the heart of religion, and makes the heart a stranger to it. Sanctifying grace is not desired, but the getting of *gain*; the honor of God is not aimed at, but growing higher in the world, the commandments of God are counted grievous things, and worldly lusts are served with delight and pleasure. Where love of the world prevails, there is a hatred of purity of heart, and strictness of life. The apostle plainly tells us, that the "friendship of the world is enmity with God," (James 4:4). His yoke, though easy, is cast off as intolerable; godliness though the greatest gain, and joined with the sweetest contentment, is looked on as unprofitable; and wisdom's ways are judged irksome, though they are truly pleasantness and peace.

5. Love of the world is the root of all evil. The apostle goes to this root, and lays it bare before our eyes; and says it is ῥίζα γὰρ πάντων τῶν κακῶν ἐστιν ἡ φιλαργυρία, the love of worldly wealth. "For the love of money is the root of all evil, which while some coveted after, they have erred from the faith, and pierced themselves through with many sorrows," (1 Timothy 6:10). Wealth itself is innocent, but the love of it is a great original sin; from where innumerable other iniquities proceed. The world having love as its power, which is the greatest commanding affection, has the whole man at command, and how wicked are the commands of it! He that is led by worldly love, into what evil ways he will go!

The robber on the highway, the burglar who breaks into houses. It is coveting and love of worldly wealth of others which is not their own, that puts them on such hazardous sins, and to theft they are resolved to add murder, rather than miss of their desired prey. How many a tradesman is as great a thief as Newgate can show; he will lie and swear and spend unwisely and eat exspensively, and worldly riches are in his heart and aim, not minding the curse that comes with dishonest gain, nor what at length he will lose by it. The love of wealth and bribes will turn judges themselves into malefactors; and make those who should be shields of the earth, to be the insufferable burdens of it. Covetousness after the treasures and grandeur of the world, has turned the church of Rome into the antichristian synagogue of Satan; and Protestant ecclesiastics who are eager after the same things, are not pastors, but spots and blemishes of the church; and go the way to overthrow it.

We used to say, *uno absurdo admisso, mille squuntur*; one absurdity being admitted, a thousand others will follow. If love of the world is allowed to reign in the heart, what sin will be disallowed, if it pretends to bring advantage and gain!

6. Love of the world subjects the soul to the power and malice of the god of the world. As the man of sin at Rome, *in ordine ad spiritualia, in the spiritual realm*, pretending spiritual authority and power, exercises great dominion over those

temporal kingdoms and nations that are deluded by him, so truly Satan the great adversary, *in ordine ad temporarlia, pretending temporal advantage*, and the good things of this world; gets and keeps under his power, all that are taken with such things as these. In whatever heart mammon reigns, it is certain that Satan sits on the throne with him. Where the world is the idol; the devil has possession of the worshipper, evil angels are called the "rulers of the darkness of this world," (Ephesians 6:12). The kingdom of the evil one is a kingdom of darkness, and by darkness it is upheld; it would spoil all, if his subjects only knew their sovereign. And this world is a great means to darken their minds, by making them to dote on it; as the Ephesians of old magnified the great goddess Diana, so they also magnify the world; as if the things of it were the greatest and best of all.

Now what secure possession the prince of this world has, where the heart is worldly; the eyes of the understanding are fast closed, and the Gospel is hidden! "But if our Gospel be hid, it is hid to them that are lost," (2 Corinthians 4:3); and what is lost for refusing Gospel light, becomes the prey of the prince of darkness. To be under his power, to be led captive by him at his pleasure, speaks great misery. He is called the old serpent, to show his subtlety, his deadly sting and poison; of old he has been man's enemy; and so will be to the world's end. He is compared to a roaring lion; to signify his mighty strength and cruelty, and outrageous hunger and eagerness to devour our souls. We read that he "deceiveth the whole world," (Revelation 12:9). All that are not called out of the world, and off from the love of it; and it is by the world itself, that he deceives them, that he may eternally destroy them.

7. The world makes them the greatest slaves of those that most love it; and this farther demonstrates the unreasonableness of this love. The greater the affection, the more absolute and perfect the subjection to it is. As love to God constrains to his service, so love to the world necessitates to slavery, and worldlings being pleased with their bondage, and fond of their fetters; they do not like, and are not likely to be set at liberty.

The world's commands are most impious and unreasonable. It commands that the Lord should be forgotten; that he should never be sought unto or minded, and accordingly we read, "The wicked through his pride will not seek after God, God is not in all his thoughts," (Psalm 10:4). It is mammon's command, that the soul and the saving of it is neglected, and the things that belong to its peace are slighted; and we read that the carnal Jews were for a temporal glorious messiah, and for a worldly kingdom, they did so; and Christ himself weeps over them for their madness and misery in so doing.

The world's injunctions are many times contrary to one another. Some worldlings are required prodigally to consume their substance on their lusts and appetites, and nothing is grudged them. They spare no cost, as if they would imitate that Roman Emperor Heliogabalus, who was infamous for his luxury and profuseness. On the contrary, some are required to save; and then as fast as they get, they lock up; and as they are very niggardly and uncharitable to others, so they are unmerciful, and will hardly allow necessaries to themselves. Such an infatuated lover of the world, (who loves it better than himself; and whose covetousness will not suffer him to enjoy the food that is in his hand; but he deprives his own soul of it) is mentioned by Solomon, "There is one alone and not a second, yea he hath neither child nor brother; yet there is no end of all his labor, neither is his eye satisfied with riches; neither saith he, for whom do I labor and bereave my soul of good? This is also vanity, yea it is a sore travail," (Ecclesiastes 4:8). The world puts its lovers on *sore travail* indeed; and whether they are for wasting or for hoarding, they lie down in sorrow at the end of their travel, being disappointed, destitute, and all their good things taken away from them.

8. In hell, what a sad and full conviction will the greediest worldlings be under, that their fondness of the world was the very height of folly! The children of the richest

are born naked into the world, as well as the offspring of the poorest; and the apostle tells us, "We brought nothing into the world and it is certain we can carry nothing out," (1 Timothy 6:7). And when the worldling's body is laid in the dust, and his face bound in secret, and his eye must no more be pleased with beautiful objects or fair prospects, his ear must no more be delighted with melody, nor his taste with rich sumptuous fare, and his place of habitation must know him no more. Alas, then it will be too late for him to know the world and himself likewise; he will then perceive that the world is a mere cheat, himself, in the worst sense a fool; and that his love being placed on that which he should have condemned, is the cause of his eternal woe.

O, what thoughts in hell, are there of these earthly things! Covetousness is there turned into anguish of conscience, and self-cursing that ever the world was coveted after. If we could hear a tongue tormented in the flame, speak of the world, what would it say? It would confess that the most desirable things on earth, are lighter than vanity and last but for a moment; but those that love and pursue them, work for themselves a far more exceeding and eternal weight of wrath and misery.

So have I demonstrated the unreasonableness of love of the world. I wish that arguments may convince you in time, that hell may not force a conviction; joined with everlasting confusion, horror and despair!

Before I come to the application, it will be very requisite to answer two queries. One, whether no love at all is allowable to the world? Two, if any love is allowable, then in what degree and manner does God allow the world to be loved?

The first query is this, whether no love at all is allowable to the world? I answer that some kind of love is allowed to it, which I prove by these *arguments:*

1. Desire is an act of love, but something of the world may be desired and prayed for, though we ought chiefly to desire the grace of God's kingdom, that we may sanctify his Name, and do his will; yet we are also taught to beg for our daily bread, and our heavenly Father will not be displeased at this, for he "knows that we stand in need of it," (Matthew 6:32). Godliness has the "promise of the life that now is," (1 Timothy 4:8) and the accomplishment of it, may without sin, be wished for. On their asking, the Lord "gives meat to them that fear him" because he "is ever mindful of his covenant," (Psalm 111:5).

Delight is also love; but the things of this world may have some delight taken in them. More things are made for delight, than for necessity; not to delight in any of these things is to act as if they were made delectable in vain. Solomon tells us, "Truly light is sweet, and a pleasant thing it is, for the eyes to behold the sun," (Ecclesiastes 11:7). It cannot be any harm to take some pleasure in that glorious luminary; and in that admirable variety of creatures which our eyes behold by the light of it. If at the same time we remember, that God is above it; and that the most excellent things of all are invisible. It is not spoken by way of condemnation but commendation of those mentioned, that in Solomon's reign, which was a time of great peace, plenty, and prosperity, as well as enjoying the privileges of the temple, they "went unto their tents joyful and glad of heart, for all the goodness that the Lord had done for David his servant, and Israel his people."

3. Love to the creatures, in a degree, is expressly commanded. To love others as ourselves is the sum of the second table of the Decalogue; this love keeping within due bounds is not a sin, but a duty and a debt. "Owe no man anything but love one another; for he that loveth another hath fulfilled the law," (Romans 13:8). We read, "So ought men to love their wives as their own bodies; he that loves his wife loveth himself; for no man ever yet hated his own flesh, but nourisheth and cherisheth it even as the Lord the church," (Ephesians 5:28-29). And, young women are to be admonished *to love their husbands and their children,*" (Titus 2:4). All love therefore towards worldly enjoyments is not forbidden. No, to be without natural affection is branded as a

great sin, against the very law and light of nature, (Romans 1:31). But it is the inordinate and over-vehement love of the world; joined with too high an esteem of it; and with a neglect of the truly excellent things which the Gospel reveals, that God is so angry at and condemns.

IN WHAT WAY DOES GOD ALLOW CHRISTIANS TO LOVE THE WORLD?

The second query is this, in what degree and manner does God allow the world to be loved? This case has need to be warily resolved; that conscience may be well informed; and show itself tender and faithful; for the heart of man being naturally inclined to the world, and no heart being quite cured of its deceitfulness; where a little is granted, a great deal is apt to be taken; and things lawful to be loved, are loved unlawfully; when love exceeds the limits that are prescribed. I answer the query in these following *particulars:*

1. The world may be loved as it is God's workmanship, and shows forth its great Creator's glory. It is a good thing with delight to study the book of nature. If we read God himself in that volume. Our minds must not terminate where our eyes do; but our understandings must clearly see by the things that are made, things invisible; even the eternal power

and Godhead of Him that made all things, "(Romans 1:20). We may love to look on the world, and to receive the blessings of it, as it is a remembrance to put us in mind of God, and a means to lead us up to Him. Creatures are now rightly refused; and are very beneficial, when they so subserve the end of their existence and donation.

2. The world may be loved as it is a means to endear the Lord who gives it. If we love God only because of the creature comforts he bestows, the creature is the end and God is the means subordinate to attain it, and this love is base, mercenary, and carnal. But if we love the creature because it helps to make our love to God himself more strong and ardent; God is pleased to see the creature so loved and used. Holy David desired and liked well enough to be delivered out of the hands of all his enemies; and of Saul, and to be settled on the throne of Israel in peace. But when he was so, a crown and kingdom was not that which he most highly valued, but he says, "I will love Thee O Lord my strength" (Psalm 18:1). He was inclined to rejoice not so much in his deliverance, as in his Deliverer that wrought it. "Then will I go to the altar of God, unto God my exceeding joy, yea on the harp will I praise thee O God my God," (Psalm 43:4).

3. The world may be loved, as it is an encouragement to religious duties and service; by doing of which, our heavenly Father is glorified. How much anger is threatened

against the children of Israel, "because they served not the Lord their God with joyfulness and gladness of heart for the abundance of all things!" (Deuteronomy 28:47). Temporal mercies may be prized and loved, and they are mercies indeed, when they are effectual motives to duty; and cause it with a cheerful liveliness to be performed. Health may be loved, that our members may be the more fit and able instruments of righteousness unto God; and we may take pleasure in the abounding of worldly blessings; if that abundance quickens us to abound in the work of the Lord, whose blessing makes rich and adds no sorrow with it.

4. The world may be loved, as it puts us into a capacity to be fruitful in good works, by which others are profited. If it is more blessed to give than to receive, as our Lord's memorable and famous saying was, (Acts 20:35), then it is lawful to desire to have, that we may give to him that needs. If providence puts us into a condition that we need to receive, we must not be discontented; but if the Lord is pleased to alter our circumstances, so that we are able to give; we should love and choose it rather. Those that have the world should do good with it, "But to do good and to communicate forget not, for with such sacrifices God is well pleased," and it is not unlawful to desire that we may have, wherewith to offer such sacrifices. Those that are rich in this world are to have a charge given to them that they are not high minded, nor trust

in uncertain riches, πλούτου ἀδηλότητι, (1 Timothy 6:17). The word signifies *obscurity* or *not being made manifest*. Riches do not appear as what they are, their vanity is usually hidden from the eyes of those that have them; and how suddenly do they many times disappear and are gone! But while they are enjoyed, they should be employed to good uses. The more the hand gets us, the more it should give; that God may be honored by the substance that is gotten, in works of piety and charity. But if your contributions this way are at the old stand and stay, that they were when you were poorer, though your estate is now very much increased; you may be grown richer, but not a better man; no certainly you are worse than formerly.

If love of the world keeps within due bounds, the wealth and good things of it will not puff us up with pride, nor be the ground of our trust and confidence; neither will the world be desired for its own sake, but that we may more abound in those works "that are good and profitable unto men," (Titus 3:8) and more beneficially serving our generation according to the will of God.

5. The world may be loved, for we may make the love of money a sin and unrighteousness, and then at length we are received into everlasting habitations, (Luke 16:9). The world is well used indeed when we make steps of the things in it, that we may the better ascend up to heaven. With our

worldly substance, acts of charity may be done to souls themselves; when by this we forward to promote and spread the Gospel, by the ministry of it. When the bowels of the saints are refreshed in us, we do our own souls a greater kindness, and they will find it turned into a very good account. What we give for the Lord's sake, he reckons as lent to himself; and by his own word, and that written, we are assured of repayment, "He that hath pity on the poor lendeth to the Lord, and that which he hath given, will he pay him gain," (Proverbs 19:17). And for all this, how glorious, though altogether free and unmerited, will be the recompense at the resurrection of the just!

The world has a loveliness in it by which we "grow rich in good works; and so lay up in store for ourselves a good foundation against the time to come, that we may lay gold on eternal life," (1 Timothy 6:19). By a good foundation, we are to understand, a good and sound evidence of our title to eternal life; for the promise of everlasting life, which is made to such good works, as the apostle mentions, is most certain, being "yea and amen in Christ," through "whom this gift of eternal life is bestowed," (Romans 6:23).

6. The world may be loved, if we care for it only so far as we have God himself with it. When the psalmist said there was none on earth that he desired besides God, he plainly signifies, that he desired no earthly thing without him. It was

a gracious expression of him who said, *Non tua satiant, nisi Tecum*, Lord! Your gifts *will never satisfy me*, unless you give me yourself with them. God is the soul as it were of every comfort, the life of all our enjoyments; everything is dead and bad without him. God, with an inheritance makes the inheritance goodly and blessed. A house is pleasant, where the Lord himself is our habitation; who is the "dwelling place of his people in all generations," (Psalm 90:1). The presence of God with the creature sanctifies it to us; there is not such a vexation, but a satisfaction and comfort in the holy use of it. A little with God is more desirable and delightful, than the greatest abundance of all manner of store without him.

7. The world may be loved, if we love it as if we loved it not; our affection being moderated by the special grace of God. Those that have the enjoyments of this life, should be as if they had none; and those that buy "as if they possessed not," (1 Corinthians 7:30). The heart must not cleave in love to that which is in the hand; but loose from it because it may quickly pass away. A man may like a commodious inn to lodge in when he is journeying; but he must not love it as a place of his constant abode. We are strangers and sojourners on earth; the world through which we are traveling must not be taking to us, as if it were our home and rest, but as leaving it, we must love it. And we must always be resolved and ready to part with the most desirable things in it, when they stand in

competition with Christ and the infinitely better, and eternally durable things of the other world.

In these particulars I have told you what that love is; which the world may have allowed to it. As the hearing of all this, the worldling perhaps may flout; perhaps you may fume and fret, and say, "It was as good that no love at all was allowed, as love thus limited." But an understanding and renewed mind will yield to what has been spoken; and grant that that love is most reasonable, that it is so moderated and spiritualized.

WORDS OF CAUTION

It will be needful to add these two words of *caution:*

First, take heed, lest mammon deceive you by transforming himself into Christ's servant; for he may do so, as well as Satan transforms himself into an angel of light. In your minding worldly affairs, take heed of pretending religion, when self is intended; it is a poor thing, a foolish part, while you profess yourselves to be Christ's; for you to lay up only for yourselves and yours. It will be your wisdom, by a faithful improvement of this world's goods, to "provide yourselves bags that wax not old, a treasure in heaven that faileth not, where no thief approacheth, neither moth corrupteth," (Luke 12:33).

Secondly, though inordinate love of the world is in some measure mortified; take heed of its again prevailing, and recovering strength in you. If you lose your first love to Christ; your old love to the world will soon revive. Be jealous over your heart and the world with a godly jealousy. Get the world more under, and let the Lord Jesus still have a high preeminence in you above all things.

THE APPLICATION

I now come to the application, and in applying this doctrine, I *shall*:

First, endeavor to convince the lovers of the world that they are indeed, such lovers.

Second, I shall dissuade such lovers from continuing as they are, by several moving considerations.

Third, I shall attempt to cast the world out of the church, and show how unbecoming the love of the world is, in professors of Christianity.

Fourth, I shall direct to the use of proper remedies and means, that this love of the world may be cured.

Fifthly, conclude with encouragement to those, in whom the love of the world is mortified.

LOVERS OF THE WORLD ARE IN FACT, LOVERS OF THE WORLD

Use 1 shall be by way of conviction. I shall endeavor to convince the lovers of the world, that they are indeed such lovers. Much has been spoken to this end already, in setting forth the love of the world, which the Word of God forbids. Seriously and faithfully try yourselves, and see whether your love to the world has those black marks and deadly signs on it, that argue you in heart and affection to be truly estranged from God. But that the convictions may be the more thorough. I shall put these following questions to you; and let conscience answer as in the Lord's presence.

1. Does the world have command of your thoughts? And cannot it command them away from God at any time, time of duty not excepted? Love has a mighty force to fix the thoughts where itself is placed. If you contentedly let mammon seize on your thoughts, when you first wake in the morning, and employ them all the day; and thoughts about the best things, as unwelcome guests, have no entertainment; if when you engage in any duty of religion at the throne of grace, in the sanctuary, or at the Lord's own table; the world without control can call away your hearts from what you are doing, and set you a thinking, projecting and contriving about

your secular affairs; certainly, though you are so expressly forbidden to "set your affection on things on the earth," (Colossians 3:2); yet on these earthly things, yours is placed, and the earthliness of your thoughts is an evidence against you.

2. Is the world the thing which you most seriously intend and aim at? What is the worldly man's chief end? Truly it is that the world may be gotten and enjoyed. God and the other world are not in his eye and design. He admires worldly wisdom above that wisdom that is spiritual, and endeavors to excel therein, that he may be shrode to get and keep the world's good things. The worldling wonders at what the apostle says, "Let no man deceive himself, if any man among you seems to be wise in this world, let him become a fool that he may be wise," (2 Corinthians 3:18). He is too wise in his own conceit to become a fool at the apostle's bidding, though all is only seeming wisdom that his is so much taken with. If the world is the principle thing with you, and above all attainments, you count it your wisdom to get the wealth and other enjoyments of it: In the catalogue of the world's lovers, your name is to be registered.

3. Are you much better pleased with worldly discourse, than that which is to edification? That passage is applicable here, "He that is of the earth, is earthly; and speaketh of the earth," (John 3:31). It is a great truth, "Out of

the abundance of the heart the mouth speaks," (Matthew 12:34). If the Word of God is in our hearts, and is loved and delighted in; "our mouths will talk of it, when we sit in the house, and when we walk by the way, when we lie down, and when we rise up," (Deuteronomy 6:6-7). But if the world has possession of the heart, the breath will smell of it; and there will be a disliking to talk or hear of anything besides.

It is to be granted, that a good man who has much earthly business to manage, may be fain to speak more words about his worldly affairs, than of God and religion; but the world is not talked of, as a thing most suitable to him. He has most pleasure in holy and gracious communication; and he often chides himself, because his tongue speaks no more of God and with no more complacency. But if your tongue can freely run on your pleasures, your pastimes, and your gain, if frothy, corrupt, and atheistic communication is not disliked; but holy counsel and cautions though you greatly need them, are very irksome, and have a harsh sound in your ears. That foolish tongue and ear of yours plainly speak and prove you to be a lover of the world.

4. Do you grudge God of the Sabbath, because then you are so much restrained, and taken off from your worldly business? Those of old who said, "When will the Sabbath be gone?" that they might sell their corn as on other days, (Amos 8:5), certainly the Sabbath was unwelcomed to them. And

they rejoiced to see the end of it; and it is apparent that the ordinances of God were condemned, "Prospering in the world and increasing in riches," was the thing they coveted. But the prophet adds, "The Lord hath sworn by the excellency of Jacob, surely I will never forget any of their works," (Amos 8:7-8). And he threatens such judgments as should set the land to trembling, and everyone to mourning that dwells in it. Heavenly minded David said, "A day in thy courts is better than a thousand," (Psalm 84:10). But lovers of the world say, "A day in the shop, at the exchange; or any place where gain is gotten, and worldly pleasure enjoyed," is much better than a thousand days in God's sanctuary. Love of the world makes a man to sign and say in his heart, "Religious duties, what a weariness are they! And why should one day in seven be thus wasted?"

5. Is your inward thought that there is much of fancy in religion; and that the things of the world are most real? The Lord complains of Israel, "I have written to them the great things of thy law; but they were counted as a strange thing," (Hosea 8:12). Hardly credible, little valuable; the truth and goodness of them by these men was very questionable. Love of the world hoodwinks the eyes of those who dote on it; so that they see little or nothing in the justifying righteousness of Christ; in partaking of the divine nature; in the graces and joys of the Holy Ghost. The young man in the Gospel, who was

drawn away from Christ by his great riches; his thought must necessarily be, that eternal life and a treasure in heaven, was doubtful, and his great possessions, as the most real and better of the two, were to be preferred. Mammon has certainly infected your heart with love, if you think that the grace and peace which believers have by Christ, and the glory they hope for, are mere imaginations; and that the psalmist did not know what he valued, or undervalued, when he said, "The law of thy mouth is better to me than thousands of gold and silver," (Psalm 119:72).

6. Do you often venture presumptuously on sin, and consequently on hell, for the *world's* sake? If the subtle tempter lays the world for the bait, does he not easily catch you? If sins that pretend to be for your worldly advantage and delight are ordinarily allowed of, your hearts are mammon's, and you are at his service, though he puts you on never such bad and wicked employment. We ought not to do evil that good may come; though the glorifying God is the good pretended, (Romans 3:7-8). But how just will the damnation of those be, who do evil, and such an evil as sin is, that the good, the sorry good of the world may come to them!

Who can conceive the infiniteness of evil that is in sin, and the misery and mischief that is in the bowels of it! The loss of heaven, the loss of souls, the terrors of death, the endless torments of hell, are all to be laid at sin's door. You are a frantic lover of the world indeed; if for the gaining and enjoying thereof, you will venture by sin to make God your enemy, and exclude you from his kingdom, and damn you to eternity!

A DISSUASION FROM BEING A LOVER OF THE WORLD

Use 2. In the second place, I am to dissuade you that are lovers of the world from continuing as you are. I wish conscience may never let you be quiet, but always be reproaching you for your fond and foolish love, and doting on that, which if your eyes were open, you would see deserves to be despised.

Arguments to move you are *these*:

1. Lovers of the world act most unworthily. True worth is not accounted by them as valuable; but mere vanity is highly esteemed. If an idiot were placed as president at the council table, above the wisest and most prudent statesman, if an errant thief were let in a tribunal, above a righteous judge, if a profane stage-player should be let into the pulpit, rather than an able and faithful preacher of the Gospel, everyone would grant that this was a most unworthy proceeding, and no regard would be had to what was really fit and worthy to be done. But worldlings act *much more* unworthily, when they

place the creatures in their hearts above the Creator, and earth has the preeminence above heaven. They are condemners of God, (Psalm 10:13) but why are they so? Is he worthy to be condemned? Can any say, "He is a barren wilderness, or a land of darkness?" (Jeremiah 2:31). What iniquity was ever found in him? (Jeremiah 2:5). But this vain world is barren, as to any substantial excellence; and the truth is, it is full of darkness and iniquity.

2. Lovers of the world are mere children in understanding. The apostle thus describes his childhood, "When I was a child, I spake as a child, I understood as a child, I thought," or reasoned ἐλογιζόμην "as a child," (1 Corinthians 13:11). Then he adds, "When I became a man, I put away childish things." So worldlings speak and understand and think of earthly things like mere children; that the trifles of this world are *grande aliquid*, some *great matter*; where if they only acted like men in understanding, they would put away those childish toys, and their own high thoughts and imaginations concerning them. The lover of the world would be wise; but worldly wisdom will never make him so. He is compared to a wild asses' colt; to show both his silliness and his obstinacy therein, (Job 11:12).

The things of the world are called ἐπίγεια *earthly things*; to show how mean and low they are; as much inferior to heavenly things in excellence, as they are in a place below them. And it is only during man's short abode on earth, that these things can be enjoyed. Yet worldlings are hugely taken, and rejoice in such things as these, as children are with rattles and counters, which grown men look on as worthless and contemptible.

3. Lovers of the world do love an enemy; and by loving it, give it power to ruin them. The apostle tells us, "Whatsoever is born of God overcometh the world," (1 John 5:4). Victory over the world plainly shows that the world wars against us; and that which wars against us is an enemy. Grace indeed can make friends of the mammon of unrighteousness; but considered in our natural state, mammon is the grand adversary. The prince of this world indeed has fiery darts of his own, which are very dangerous; and we have need of the shield of faith to quench them. But some of the worst weapons which he uses against us, are drawn forth out of the world's armory. It was said, as I remember, to a king of Macedon, that he *should fight with silver spears*, and he would certainly be victorious. Satan goes this way. He uses the wealth, the pleasure, and grandeur of the world as his weapons; and how mighty are these carnal weapons found! What multitudes are conquered by them!

Worldlings should remember that what they love, Satan makes use of as an instrument of death; that by this means they may be destroyed. What an absurd thing it would be for a man to be fond of a dagger that is to stab him, or of a poison that is to be given to him! And truly Satan does as effectually dispatch souls by the things of the world; as lives are taken away by poniard or poison. Contempt of the world would prevent mischief by it, and frustrate the wiles of the evil one; but love of the world makes it so dangerous and deadly, and the things of it become strong cords to draw men away from God, and to hale them away to eternal perdition.

4. Love of the world fills it with sin and wickedness. Worldly lusts vehemently urge men to aim at nothing, though never so bad, for their satisfaction! We read, "From whence come wars and fightings among you? Come they not hence, even of your lusts that war in your members?" (James 4:1). Men do fight for the world; they swear and lie for the world; they cast off religion and the fear of God for the world. Desire after something or other in this world and you will find yourself at the bottom of the most wicked villainies that are acted in it! In 1 Kings 21:12-13, we find a fast proclaimed religion mostly abused; Naboth set on high among the people, as a notorious, impious traitor and malefactor; two sons of belial, like our late Irish evidences, witness against him that he blasphemed, and he is carried forth out of the city, and stoned with stones that he died; and the ground of all this horrid wickedness is Ahab's coveting of Naboth's vineyard.

5. Love of the world loads it with judgments and calamities. It causes men to neglect the God of heaven, and the duty which they owe him; and by it they provoke his wrath and indignation against them. And this displeasure breaks forth in diverse plagues and miseries; "The Lord will make thy plagues wonderful, and the plagues of thy seed; even great plagues and of long continuance," (Deuteronomy 28:58). How terribly does he speak, "My determination is to gather the nations, that I may assemble the kingdoms, to pour on them my indignation, even all my fierce anger; for all the earth shall be devoured with the fire of my jealousy," (Zephaniah 3:8).

And as lovers of the world incur God's hatred, so it oftentimes makes them full of hatred, envy, and unjust and uncharitable designs one against another. Worldly love breaks through all natural and civil bonds, as well as obligations in point of conscience. Our Lord therefore says, "Beware of men;" as now being very dangerous creatures to one another. And the prophet says, "Take ye heed everyone of his neighbor, and trust ye not in any brother; for every brother will utterly supplant, and every neighbor will walk with slanders; and they will deceive everyone his neighbor, and will not speak the truth; they have taught their tongue to speak lies, they are very artificial at it, and weary themselves to commit iniquity."

An ambitious affectation of rule and governing, and worldly wealth and greatness; was the rise of the four monarchs mentioned in Daniel 7:3, compared to the four great beasts. And by these beasts, how many were devoured! With what brutish rage and cruelty were these kingdoms managed! It was a true observation of an ancient father, *Omnes nos sumus, aut corvi qui lacerant, aut cadavera qua lacerantur. All are either birds of prey, or a prey to these birds.* Misery is great on the earth, for the subtle prey on the simple; and the stronger devour the weaker. Love of the world and self-love make men savage and cruel to one another.

6. Lovers of the world help forward their own affliction. A high esteem of the world raises expectation to a great height; and when it does not answer expectation; but comes exceedingly short of it, there is the greater trouble in the disappointment. The stronger the worldling's affections are, the sharper affliction is; the more grievous are the crosses he meets with, and the losses which he sustains. Love excites those other passions of sorrow, wrath, envy, and care which have a great deal of torment in them. The world is rightly compared to sharp thorns, to a pricking briar; why should any be so desirous to hug thorns and briars and brambles in his heart! The strength of our affections and passions make earthly things thus piercing to us; where if these affections were only mortified, we should not be liable to such disturbance, but with the apostle we "should know how to

want and how to abound, and learn in whatsoever state we are therewith to be content," (Philippians 4:12).

7. Love of the world is a great hindrance to faith in Christ Jesus. This is it which keeps the heart fast shut against the Lord of life, the Author of eternal salvation. It is written, "How can ye believe which receive honor one of another, and seek not the honor that cometh from God only?" (John 5:44). If affecting honor in the world, and glory from men, makes believing impossible; by parity of reason, affecting worldly delights and wealth, while such affection is indulged; will be as effectual impediment to faith. By the marriage supper, (Matthew 22:2) we are to understand the benefits of Christ, which the Gospel invites all to partake of; and the word marriage, gives a hint, that they who would partake of these benefits, must consent to be betrothed to him; but when the invitation was made, they who were invited, made light of it, (verse 5) and minding and being taken with the things of the world was the reason, it is said, they went their way, one to his farm, and another to his merchandise.

The young man in the Gospel was inclined towards Christ; and one would have thought, was near this spiritual marriage; but love of the world forbade the banes. He could not be brought to prefer Christ and heaven, before his earthly riches, which he had such a store of. Agrippa was "almost persuaded to be a Christian," (Acts 26:28) but we never read that he was persuaded altogether; and it is more than probable that love of worldly greatness was the obstacle: we do not read that he was willing to hazard his crown of gold, and take up the cross of Christ, though he might have gained a crown of life. Love of the world is opposite to the great command of the Gospel, which is to believe! True faith overcomes the world, and this victory is by throwing it, and the love of it out of the heart, or else Christ would never be received there.

8. The greatest lovers of the world may have the soonest, and will have the saddest parting with it. The worldling may be suddenly arrested by death, the king of terrors, and brought before that dreadful tribunal, where he will be both judged and condemned together. In the midst of a worldly and selfish design, in the very heart and eagerness of his spirit towards his earthly business; when he promises to himself so much time in "such a place, to buy and sell, and get gain," (James 4:13). His life may prove a vapor which suddenly vanishes away; and then all his thoughts and projects perish; and when his breath goes forth and he returns to the earth; it will be found that he has been laboring for the wind.

And how sad a parting with the world will the lover of it have! Clothes and ornaments must be put off, and the winding sheet must be put on; delicious fare, and costly wines must be tasted no more; Sleep is a locking up of the senses, but death will destroy them; and what is pleasing to the senses, must be enjoyed no longer. The dearest relations must be bid farewell , without hopes of sending any of them from the dead, to warn them to repent: The pleasant habitation with all its furniture and delights must be left, and he must lie down in a dark and cold grave. But O, there is one part of him, which death cannot seize; and that is his soul, and where must that go? Hell is the place that will receive the separated spirits of all those that die in their worldliness and wickedness; "The wicked shall be turned into hell, and all the nations that forget God," (Psalm 9:17).

Let all this which has been spoken, cause these lovers of the world to bethink themselves; that they may perceive that there is the worst sort of frenzy in that earthly affection which is so predominant in them.

But some may here object that speaking this way against the love of the world, may prove of very ill and dangerous consequence. If the world may not be coveted after then merchandise must cease; and trading is under great discouragement; the endeavors of all will be damped in the works of their particular callings; and money that is said to answer all things will signify little or nothing. If worldly gain may be no more minded than had been allowed; the seaman will have little heart to sail; and the soldier will have less courage to fight for his king, and country; and so in the long run, this doctrine which teaches contempt of the world may undermine the throne, and prove prejudicial to the state and government.

To this objection I answer: That if love to the world is moderated by the Word, and God is loved above all, righteousness followed after, and the world to come chiefly minded, all the harms consequent on it, are only the mere imaginations of a foolish, carnal mind. Godliness will be found profitable for all things; hurtful neither to any person or thing in the whole world.

The merchant whose soul is truly wise and noble, that is to say, is heavenly, so that he looks principally after the pearl of great price, (Matthew 13:46), he goes the way to have a blessing on his other merchandise; and he is more fit to be trusted with more of the world; because he and all that he has, are sincerely at God's service. The just and righteous tradesman, whose desire is to render to God the things that are God's, and loves him and his service before anything in the world; who does not wrong his neighbor by any false and knavish dealings; and is ready to show him mercy when he needs it. The Lord delights in such a man. "A false balance is an abomination to the Lord, but a just weight is his delight," (Proverbs 11:1). "He loves him that followeth after righteousness. He rejoiceth over him to do him good," (Proverbs 15:9), and takes pleasure in his prosperity. How can such a man be the least prejudiced by his seeking of God, since there is such a sure promise; that "they that seek the Lord shall not want any good thing," (Psalm 34:10).

The seaman, who loves the Lord above the world, and trusts in him; and desires so much of earthly things, and no more than divine wisdom, sees expedient for him to have, this man is safest in his sailing, the providence of God is his convoy, the Anchor of his hope is cast within the veil: His dependence shall not be in vain; for the Lord is the "confidence of them that are afar off on the sea," (Psalm 65:5) and even the wind and the sea obey him. And if anything adverse befalls him; it shall work for good, and issue in his greater advantage.

The soldier who has good cause, and a good conscience, who seeing the hazard and uncertainty of life, is weaned from the world, and makes sure of heaven; this man is "compassed with the favor of God as with a shield," (Psalm 5:12). How valiantly will such a soldier fight against the enemy, who has the Lord of hosts, the God of battle to stand by him! An army of such soldiers both by sea and land, what a security they would be to the throne and government! Where a covetous, wicked and debauched army, large offers of gold may easily make them unfaithful; and an evil conscience, when it comes to engagement with the enemy, may make them cowardly and fainthearted; and there are so many accursed things among them, as may justly provoke the Lord to deny them victory!

Do not let the rulers and potentates of the earth look on Christianity with a jealous eye, because it persuades all men to despise the world; for Christians indeed, who set their hearts on, and seek the things above, will make the best use of things on earth; and in using them will most consult the public good, and prove general blessings to all, and that from the mightiest to the meanest.

Do the Poor Love the World?

In the next place some may also object: That all this discourse against the love of the world, concerns them either not at all, or only very little; for they are poor, and have very little of the world to set their hearts on. The rich and wealthy indeed may need caution, but those who have so small a portion of the world, are in no danger.

To this I return an answer: That the poor of the world may be over-lovers of the world. And they who have very little of the world, may be eternally undone by it.

1. The poor of the world may *over-love* the world. Their little may be very greatly esteemed, and have a large share of their affections. They may love one pound as well, as a very wealthy man may love a thousand. If the poor are

discontented, and fret at providence, that they have no more of the world; this discontent discovers an inordinate affection to the world. If they are envious at those who have more than themselves, it argues that the world is too lovely and excellent in their eyes; and they do not consider that the most prosperous worldlings "shall soon be cut down as the grass, and wither as the green herb," (Psalm 37:2). If the poor are eager in their desires after wealth, though they cannot obtain what they desire, this desire is covetousness; though what is coveted flees from them, and their most diligent pursuits after it are in vain.

The world may have a full possession of the heart, the thoughts, the admiration, the choice and most eager affections of it; and yet perhaps very little of the world may ever come into the hands.

2. They who have very little of the world may be eternally undone by it. Therefore, even these have need to be cautioned against the love of it. If the poor man's care about the world, and desire after it, takes him off from holy duties, or makes him very heartless in them. If he so minds his small and petty concerns in the world, as to be mindless of his soul, and to neglect the salvation of it. Though he has never so little of the world, he is very much a worldling; and how inexcusable he is, who for so small a matter of the world, will venture to lose his soul; the loss of which, the gain of "the

whole world is not enough to compensate!" (Mark 8:36-37). Judas was far from being a rich man; he bare the bag after Christ; and his heart was too much in it; for so small a matter as thirty pieces of silver, he betrayed his Lord, he undid himself, and became the son of eternal perdition, (John 17:12). If a poor man will speak and act falsely and dishonestly to get a penny; he loves the world with a witness, who will presume to sin against God for the gain of it. He loves it in such a high degree, that he really hates himself for the sake of it.

CASTING THE WORLD OUT OF THE CHURCH

Use 3. In the third place, I shall attempt to cast the world out of the church, and show how unbecoming the love of the world is, in professors of Christianity. The very heathens, by the light of nature, may see the world's vanity; and many of them did discern that virtue, and goodness, and future rewards in the other world, were much more desirable. The poet cries out with passion, *O curva in terras anima, & cowlwarium inanes!* Alas, that souls should be so bowed down towards the earth, as if there were no heaven over their heads! And if the light of nature makes the heathen's love the world to be without apology; the light of the Gospel, which gives such a view of the world to come, causes this love of the world in professors of religion, to be much more without excuse. Now that the heart of everyone who names the name of Christ, may come out from the world, and love it no longer; let these following particulars be pondered with the greatest seriousness.

1. How little of the world did Christ himself have in the days of his flesh, and how much did he condemn it! When the people would have forced a crown on him, and made a king of him, he refused it, (John 6:15). No, when Satan offered him all the imperial diadems and kingdoms of the world, and the glory of them, how far was he from accepting them! (Matthew 4:10). He that was Lord of all, became poor, and was so contented to be so, "that we through his poverty might be rich," (2 Corinthians 8:9). As his poverty and sufferings were meritorious of the best things for us, so the eyeing of Christ's poverty, as to the things of the world, may be a strong inducement to make us despise an earthly treasure, and mind the true riches, the worth of which is unsearchable. Shall Christ the Head show such a contempt of the world, and shall not the same mind be in them that profess themselves to be his members?

2. What strict cautions our Lord gives against coveting this present world! He very well knew both our natural proneness to be eager after it, and our great peril in being so. He understood the earthliness of our hearts; therefore he says,

"Lay not up for yourselves treasures on earth," (Matthew 6:19) he forbids "laboring for the meat which perisheth," (John 6:27). It must not be our greatest labor to get the things of the world which are of a perishing nature, and which cannot prevent our perishing forever; but we must labor for that meat which endures to everlasting life. Eternal life must be minded chiefly, and the means to obtain it; and this life is to be had in Christ; for him "hath God the Father sealed."

What a caution it is, "Take heed and beware of covetousness; for a man's life consisteth not in the abundance of the things which he possesseth," (Luke 12:15). The words translated, "Take heed and beware," are Ὁρᾶτε καὶ φυλάσσεσθε, *see and look well*; and guard and keep yourselves from covetousness. See the emptiness of what you covet after. See the sin and provocation there is in covetousness; and be sure to keep yourselves from that which will do you so little good, and which will be so great an evil to you.

3. Those that enter into covenant with God, profess to renounce the world. Professors of Christianity have been baptized in the Name of the true God, Father, Son, and Holy Ghost. And as the Israelites of old entered into covenant with God in their very infancy, and were by their circumcision the "token of that covenant," (Genesis 17:11) laid under an obligation to love and serve the Lord Jehovah. In like manner, under the new testament, baptism is an engagement of such a

nature. From their very infancy, the offspring of Christian parents are "holy," (1 Corinthians 7:14) separated to the Lord, and devoted to him. And they that are thus consecrated and devoted to God, why should mammon have their love and labor? As they are bound to abstain from the evil of sin, and to resist the evil one; so to keep their hearts off from the world, that the Lord may have their hearts for himself to dwell in; and their whole man to be employed in that work to which he calls them. Every time professors renew covenant with God, they freshly renounce the world; and what perfidiousness and covenant breaking it is, if they shall dote on it!

In the Old Testament, idolatry was accounted as a gross, covenant-breaking with the true God. Therefore he says to idolatrous Israel, *Loammi* you are *not my people*; and *Loruhamah*, I will "no more have mercy on you," (Hosea 1:6,9). Now covetousness being expressly called idolatry; the covetous professor violates his covenant with the Lord, and desires the world. It may startle all to read, that "covetousness is idolatry," and "that for this thing's sake the wrath of God cometh on the children of disobedience," (Colossians 3:5-6).

4. O how the love of the world casts a blemish on professors of religion! How it debases both their spirits and their practices, when they are so intent on earthly gain; when they inquire so seriously, who will show them any worldly good? They speak, they act, they walk just like other men; and

show themselves of the same worldly spirit with them. How unlovely these spots of the world make professors! This text is also applicable, "They have corrupted themselves, their spot is not the spot of his children, they are a perverse and crooked generation," (Deuteronomy 32:5). This love of the world argues whether a lack of faith, or a great weakness of faith in them; and it hardens those that are outside, in their worldly-mindedness and infidelity. How can the profane choose except to be confirmed in their high thoughts of earth, and their low thoughts of heaven; when they evidently perceive professors, in the whole course of their endeavors, so much neglecting heaven for earth's sake!

I do not wonder that the covetous, considering what harm they do by discrediting religion; that they are ranked with some of the worst of men in Scripture. When you have a pack of very bad men mentioned together, you shall find that the Holy Spirit thrusts the covetous in among them, "Be not deceived, neither fornicators, nor idolaters, nor adulterers, nor effeminate, nor abusers of themselves with mankind, nor thieves, nor covetous, nor drunkards, nor revilers, nor extortioners, shall inherit the kingdom of God," (1 Corinthians 6:9-10). Also, "But now I have written unto you not to keep company; if any man that is called a brother, a fornicator or covetous, or an idolater, or a railer, or a drunkard, or an extortioner; with such an one do not to eat," (1 Corinthians 5:11).

5. Love of the world is the schismatic, the great church-render and divider. Schisms have made sore wounds in the church of Christ; and carnal and worldly minds have caused them, "For whereas there is among you envying, and strife, and divisions; are ye not carnal and walk as men?" (1 Corinthians 3:3). In these divisions, whatever order, or decency, or purity, is pretended, some carnal and worldly interest is at the bottom. Schismatic Diotrephes will not receive the brethren; and casts those that were better than himself out of the church. The reason is, he is fond of "honor from men, and loves to have the preeminence," (3 John 1:9-10). Therefore perverse men speak "perverse things, that they may draw away disciples after them?" (Acts 20:30). The apostle tells us that they are acted by the "hope and love of worldly gain;" they "teach things which they ought not, for filthy lucre's sake," (Titus 1:11).

Breaches among Christians at this day, are wide as the sea. Fountains of tears are not sufficient to bewail them. And mammon has a great hand in them. If men can only keep up their own repute in the world; and that of their party; if they can only feather their own nests; how careless and unconcerned many are of what becomes of the general interest of the Christian religion! If professors of all persuasions would only deny themselves as to their secular interest; if they would only love the world less, and one another more; if in honor they would seek the wealth of others, as well as their own; and consider that divisions in the house of God, have a tendency to the destruction and fall of it; we might hope then to see our breaches healed; this would be the way to unity and peace.

6. Love of the world is the great cause of *apostasy* in the hour of temptation. It was this love which cast down two stars from heaven; it made Judas to fall first, and Demas after him, "Demas hath forsaken me having loved this present world," (2 Timothy 4:10). Fear of the world's fury makes many apostates; but with that fear, love is joined; they over affect their worldly comforts, and will not part with them for Christ's sake. The Pythagoreans were want to set up κανόταφια, *empty coffins* in the room of those who had degenerated from their philosophy; as being apostates from a good life, which is the true life indeed; and therefore fit to be reckoned among the dead. Ah, how many empty coffins might be set up in the room of apostatized professors in this degenerate and backsliding age! And on these coffins there might be this inscription, "These fell from the faith, and departed from God, being drawn away by love to the world."

REMEDIES FOR CURING LOVE TO THE WORLD

Use 4. In the fourth place, I am to direct to proper remedies for the curing of this love of the world, I hope by this you apprehend the malignity and danger of this disease.

The remedies that are to be prescribed against it are *these*:

1. Pray earnestly to be delivered from the spirit of this world. The apostle speaks of πνεῦμα τοῦ κόσμου, the spirit of the world which he would "not entertain," (1 Corinthians 2:12). Those that are acted by this spirit, judge nothing to have worth in it, but what is visible and sensible; as for spiritual things they are counted foolishness. No, he wrote that leviathan was sunk so deep into the flesh, that he asserted, the notion of a spirit implied a contradiction. The spirit of the world is perpetually commending the things of it, as if these alone were substantial, other things being mere dreams and shadows. The body is looked on as the man; and the satisfaction of the bodies' appetites and desires; is esteemed the very height of humane felicity. Look on such infirmities as most false and pernicious, for if they are entertained, they will chain your hearts to the earth; the world which is nothing, will be all; Christ, who is all, will be nothing to you. Look upward to the Father of lights, and entreat that the light in

you may not be darkness; that the world may never have your judgments to side with it; nor pronounce that it is the best thing for you.

2. Take heed of being swayed and led away by the general example. You are not to follow a multitude to do evil; neither must you imitate a multitude in casting away your love on vanity. The sons of men are strongly induced to love the world by the general example that is before their eyes; the hearts of most, they see, are eager this way; and by it they harden one another in their worldly-mindedness. A few indeed are chosen out of the world; and these choose and seek a better world; but the generality of men everywhere are earthly; the shrewdest heads, the greatest wits, the deepest politicians, and many times clergymen of the highest rank and order, mind the *earth*, and deride heaven; and no wonder that their example has a mighty influence, and many follow their pernicious ways.

The apostle tells us, that "Not many wise men after the flesh, not many mighty, not many noble are called," (1 Corinthians 1:26) and since the things on earth are so generally in request; and that among the wise, the mighty, and noble of the world, you had need greatly to beware, lest your hearts and affections be carried away by the strong and mighty stream of such examples. Why should you do as the most do? Why should you love what the most love, since all considered in their natural state, "lie in wickedness, and are void of understanding?" And, "There is none righteous, no not one; there is none that understandeth, there is none that seeketh after God," (Romans 3:10-11). The world is a great bedlam; most in it are perfectly mad for love of it. Oh, cry to be renewed in the spirit of your mind, that you may not be besides yourselves as they are!

3. See the insufficiency of all the wealth in the world to redeem a lost soul, "Forasmuch as ye know ye were not redeemed with corruptible things, as silver and gold, but with the precious blood of Christ, as of a lamb without blemish, and without spot," (1 Peter 1:18-19). Gold and silver are vilified, called corruptible; these cannot be a price for a sinner's ransom; but the blood of Christ is precious indeed; with this price, all souls that are saved are bought. Would you cease loving the world? See how unable it is to help you in your greatest misery. Behold yourselves to be compassed about with innumerable evils, and your iniquities taking hold of you; and making your hearts to fail within you; (Psalm 40:12). Take notice of the justice of God demanding satisfaction for all your offenses; with the wrath of God hanging over your heads, and the curse of the broken law lying on you; and in this greatest distress, what can poor mammon do for your help? Nothing of the world can prevent a soul's sinking into hell, nor pacify and heal a wounded

conscience. When Judas' conscience was full of anguish and horror, for his sinning in betraying innocent blood, he casts away the pieces of silver which he had coveted; (Matthew 27:4-5) the greatest treasure in such a case is unavailable.

4. Reflect on your own experience, and often recall what you have found the world to be in you. The book of Ecclesiastes is a declaration of Solomon's experience of this world. God *suffered* him to enjoy a great deal of it, that his experience might be larger; and reflecting, on so full a trial he had found it to be, his disparaging of it shows how little he loved and admired it. Those expressions, "vanity of vanities," and "vanity increased," and "vexation of spirit," and "no profit," and "labor with sore travel," and "evil disease," speak *plainly* of the mortification of worldly affection. And what does your own experience tell you when you consult it? When did the world answer your expectation? When did you find in it that which you hoped for? When you have trusted in it, how has it failed you! You have been rewarded with vanity, and how vain has your conscience proved! "Let not him that is deceived trust in vanity; for vanity shall be his recompense," (Job 15:31). No, that worldly enjoyment, which you have been most fond of, has been found to deserve it least, and has proved the greatest cross to you. Let sense and feeling of the world's thorns cure your love to it, as if it were an easy and pleasant thing.

5. Improve the crucifixion of Christ. Our Lord on the cross spoiled Satan, and triumphed over him. He silenced him as an accuser; and the virtue of his death is too strong for him as a tempter. The old Adam was also crucified with Christ, that the whole body of sin might be destroyed. And mammon, in a sense, was nailed to the cross of Christ also. And if you behold him hanging on that tree; his bewitching and ensnaring power is gone; you may glory in the cross, and over mammon. "God forbid that I should glory, save in the cross of our Lord Jesus Christ, by whom the world has been crucified unto me, and I unto the world," (Galatians 6:14). The world was crucified to the apostle; for he looked on it as a great deceiver, which seduces souls from the way of truth and righteousness; he looked on it as under a curse: And as the Jews looked on Christ when they crucified him, so the apostle looked on the world, as "having no form of comeliness, no beauty in it, to make it desirable." The apostle also was crucified to the world. His love to the world was killed, and he was dead to the things of the world that were most enticing, and most alluring.

It is one great work, and a great piece of skill in faith, to fetch power from Christ's crucifixion, to crucify worldly lusts and desires. This is done by eyeing the purpose of Christ in dying; and the purchase he has made by his death; and by relying on the blood of the everlasting covenant. The purpose and design of Christ in dying was, that he might take away servants and slaves to mammon; and bring them to God, that having their fruit to holiness, the end might be everlasting life; and our Lord, by his death, has purchased sufficient grace to spiritualize the affections of the merest worldling on the face of the earth; and in the everlasting covenant which is ratified by his blood, we find a promise of the Spirit, who by his powerful working, makes us to be conformable to Christ's death; so that we are dead to, and unmoved by the biggest offers the world can make to us. And this Spirit instructs us to know the "far greater and more glorious things which are freely given to us of God," (1 Corinthians 2:12).

6. Be very desirous to know the power of the Lord Jesus' resurrection. The first Adam sinned as a public person, and representative of his whole progeny; and they all fell with him in his first transgression. They also derive from him a corrupt nature, a low spirit, which most strongly and sinfully inclines them to earthliness and sensuality. The second Adam also rose and ascended as a public person, and representative of all believers; and as his representing believers in heaven, is an assurance that they will at last come to him; so from him they derive a new nature; an elevated spirit; so that nothing in the world can satisfy them; it is towards heaven that their new hearts are inclined, and that God, who is gloriously present there. Christ's resurrection is not only to put us in

mind how much it is our duty and interest to rise with him; but his resurrection is powerful and mighty to make us do so. Our Lord who is risen, indeed, shows himself alive in believer's hearts, "Christ lives in me," (Galatians 2:20) the apostle says. They shake off the dust of the earth; and by that "working by which he is able to subdue all things to himself," it comes to pass that their conversation and affection is in heaven, (Philippians 3:20).

The apostle desired to know Christ better, and more to experience the "power of his resurrection," (Philippians 3:10). Let your desires be the same; and this power will subdue your love to the world; and the Spirit of him who raised Christ from the dead, will quicken and raise your spirits, and set them on things above. We read, "But God who is rich in mercy, for the great love wherewith he loved us, even when we were dead in sins, hath quickened us together with Christ; by grace are ye saved; and hath raised us up together, and made us sit together, and made us sit together in heavenly places in Christ Jesus," (Ephesians 2:4-6). This rising is with Christ; and so is the sitting in heavenly places. It is "as a shadow and continueth not." In this world he has only a very short continuance indeed. Serious thoughts of leaving the world may be a great means to cure the love of it. Death is perpetually making nearer approaches to you; and every day that passes over your heads, you have one less day than you had, to be in this world and to enjoy it. How soon will the house of clay fall to the ground! How soon "will the dust return to the earth as it was!" (Ecclesiastes 12:7). Meditate much of yourselves returning to the earth; and earthly things will appear so poor and fading, that they will no longer be affected.

"O death! Thou art the worldling's horror and the world's disparagement! Thou stainest the glory of the greatest: Thou spoilest the beauty of the fairest: Thou takest away all the treasures of the wealthiest in the world, and none is able to withstand thee!" When the richest men, the glory of whose houses is more increased, come to die, they shall carry nothing of all that they possess away with them, for, "their glory shall not descend after them," (Psalm 49:17).

And as you are to think much of your own latter end, so also think much of the end of this world. It is "reserved unto fire against the day of judgment and perdition of ungodly men," (2 Peter 3:7). Burning to death is a punishment inflicted on those that are guilty of the sin of witchcraft. This world which has bewitched so many millions of souls, will at length be burned; "The heavens will pass away with a great noise, and the elements will melt with fervent heat, and the earth and the works that are therein shall be burnt up," (2 Peter 3:10). By faith, see this entire world in flames; all the things that are in it, and the glory of them quite consumed; this is the way to have worldly love extinguished.

9. Let hopes of heaven be lively and beg some foretastes of it. Let Christ himself be received by faith into your hearts; and being and ruling in you, let him be the foundation of your "hope of glory," (Colossians 1:27) and this hope will make you to resemble him in purity, "Every man that hath this hope in him, purifieth himself even as He is pure," (1 John 3:3); and you will be kept from the defilements of the unrighteous mammon. See the glory of the great and holy Jerusalem, adorned as a bride for the bridegroom. The city is said to "be of pure gold, and the foundations of the wall garnished with all manner of precious stones," (Revelation 21:18-19). The most valuable things in nature are but faint metaphors to set forth its surpassing excellence. No night shall be there, either of darkness or of sorrow, but an eternal day and joy. The city will "have no need of the sun or moon to shine in it; for the glory of the Lamb is the light thereof." No sin or curse will be there; all that come to that blessed place, shall see the face of God, and that sight will satisfy them with his likeness; and what a beautiful and glorious thing will the Image of God be, when it is perfectly restored! "And they shall reign forever and ever," (Revelation 21:32, 22:4-5). Hope of all this glory will set you to longing for it; it will obscure this world, and cure your foolish and fond love to it; especially if

you have some present foretastes of what is to be your eternal feast hereafter; and the comforting Spirit, by his joys that are unspeakable and full of glory; is the earnest to you of that incomparable inheritance.

10. See what is more worthy of your love, than this world is. Anything of God, of Christ, deserves it better; his word, his ways, and his ordinances. But of your love, the Lord himself is *most* worthy. Desire that he would cause his goodness and glory to pass before you; and thereby carry your hearts and affections quite away from this evil world. It was the request of Moses, "Lord I beseech thee show me thy glory!" (Exodus 33:18). Such a sight will work wonders in any heart. How vain and foul will mammon appear, when the glory of God is thus made manifest! Take notice how saints in Scripture set their hearts. Abraham, the father of the faithful, Isaac and Jacob, the heirs with him of the same promise, "confessed they were strangers and pilgrims on earth, and looked for a city that hath foundations whose builder and maker is God," (Hebrews 11:10, 13). Moses refused Egypt's glory, its treasures, its pleasures, and its very crown; his love was placed on the invisible God, as the best and most exceeding reward. As the world was not worthy of such saints, so they counted it not worthy of their hearts; they are witnesses of this world's undesirableness, and are a cloud to direct your steps towards the heavenly Canaan. Be of the same

mind with them, and pray that your hearts "may be directed into the love of God, and patiently waiting for Christ Jesus," (2 Thessalonians 3:5).

ENCOURAGING BELIEVERS

Use 5. In the last place, I shall encourage sincere believers in whom the love of this world is mortified. The grounds of encouragement are these.

1. As you are not lovers of the world, so you do not need to fear it. All attempts of the world to frighten, to seduce, to corrupt, to take away your crown from you, shall be frustrated, "Ye are God's little children, and have overcome them, because greater is He that is in you, than he that is in the world," (1 John 4:4).

2. Your heavenly Father knows what of this world you need, and without your coveting or solicitude will certainly provide what he sees to be indeed best for you. You may live by faith, and depend on him who is the possessor of heaven and earth; he has enough in his hand for you; and how much love in his heart towards you! You shall be provided for when it is unlikely. "In the days of famine you shall be satisfied," (Psalm 37:19). When the "fig tree does not blossom, and there is no fruit in the vine, when the labor of the olive fails, and the field yields no meat; the flock is cut off from the fold, and

there is no herd in the stalls; even then you may rejoice in the Lord, and joy in the God of your salvation," (Habakkuk 3:17-18). No, the Lord, whom you love above the world, will not only spread your table, and fill your cups, but he will spread his own table for you, he will "abundantly satisfy you with the fatness of his house, and make you drink of the rivers of his pleasure," (Psalm 36:8).

3. Sitting loose from the world, your provisions are not only sure, but are sanctified and blessed to you. A little with a blessing from heaven is better than the greatest abundance and a curse on all of it. The riches of many worldly-minded men are not so good as the food conveniently provided for one righteous man, (Psalm 37:16). The good man's prayer, and God's promise makes every creature of God good to him; and a holy use of it is made. "Every creature of God is good, and nothing to be refused, if it be received with thanksgiving, for it is sanctified by the word of God and prayer," (1 Timothy 4:4-5). When the Lord himself shall say to a saint, "Much good may thy food do thee, which I give thee!" What a relish this adds to it!

4. Not loving the world, but the Father above it; what manifestations you will have of his Fatherly love to you! Mercies may be looked on as tokens of his love; and afflictions too. "For whom the Lord loveth he correcteth, even as a father to the son in whom he delighteth," (Proverbs 3:12). In your

own houses and closets and in his house; in secret duties and public ordinances, the Lord will be ready to "manifest himself to you, as he does not manifest himself to the world," (John 14:22). And the joy you have will be because of the most plentiful harvest of gladness which is the effect of the light of his countenance.

5. Not loving the world, you will at last go more easily and joyfully out of it. It is love to this earth that makes men so loathe to depart; not only because of what they love, are they unwilling to leave; but also because they have just ground to fear, that evil things in the next world abide them. But he who has counted all things in the world to be loss, that he might gain Christ; he may desire to be dissolved that he may be with Christ, which is far better, (Philippians 1:23). The more worldly love is mortified, the more the heart and treasure at present is in heaven; when you leave the earth, the more abundant entrance will be administered to you in the heavenly kingdom.

What are the pleasures here? Entertainment, food and fare of happiness, foolish night fires and gatherings, women's and children's wishes, guilded emptiness, shadows well-mounted, dreams in a career, embroidered lies, money, extravagance, dreams of all kinds; these are the pleasures here.

True earnest sorrows, rooted miseries, anguish in making ends meet, vexations ripe and blown, sure-footed griefs, solid calamities, plain demonstrations, evident and clear, fetching their proofs even from the very bone; these are the sorrows here.

But O! the folly of distracted men! As poets have said, *Who grieves in earnest, joys in jest, foolish things you still pursue. Preferring like brute beasts a loathsome den, before a court, even that extravagance which is above others and so clear. Instead, search for where there are no sorrows, but delights more true, than miseries here!*

ASKING AMISS IN PRAYER

"Ye ask and receive not because ye ask amiss, that ye may consume it on your lusts," (James 4:3).

In the latter end of the foregoing chapter of James, the apostle commends that wisdom which is from above, that is first pure, then peaceable, gentle and easy to be entreated; that is, without partiality and hypocrisy, full of mercy and good fruits. Fruits that are good and beneficial both to the church and to the world. In the beginning of this chapter, he inveighs against wars and contentions, and affirms that they are bad in their effects, and in their causes. They are bad in their effects; producing many sinful disorders, acts of violence, cruelty, injustice, and all manner of wickedness. Bad also in their causes, for "from whence come wars and fightings among you? Come they not hence, even of your lusts that war in your members?"

Not that all war is to be condemned; for sometimes the ambition, covetousness, and wrath of men, and their insatiable desire of domination and ruling make a defensive war against them to be necessary. We read in Scripture, that wars have been waged in faith. Believers, by "faith, out of weakness were made strong, waxed valiant in sight, turned to flight the armies of the aliens." And some are of an opinion that mystical Babylon, by fire and sword shall at last be utterly destroyed.

Yet notwithstanding, peace is a thing that ought with the greatest earnestness to be pursued by all that profess subjection to the Gospel and Prince of peace. And indeed the apostle shows a better way to obtain our desires, than by fighting; and that is by praying. We shall gain more by wrestling with God, than by warring with men. "Ye lust and have not; ye kill and desire to have, and cannot obtain; ye fight and war, yet ye have not because ye ask not." But all asking is not prevailing; there is a prayer that becomes sin; there is an asking which obtains not a grant, but a denial; and of this the text speaks, "Ye ask and receive not because ye ask amiss, that ye may consume it on your lusts."

In the text, these particulars are to be *observed*:

First, here is a duty, and that is asking: I grant that it is a privilege to have liberty to ask; but it is also often pressed and incumbent on us as a duty; and to neglect it is the greater of both fault and folly.

Second, this duty we find was unsuccessful, "Ye ask and receive not." Prayer turned no account; many words were spoken, and labor bestowed, and time spent in vain. That God whom they prayed to was not pleased; they themselves were not profited by their supplications.

Third, the reason of prayers unsuccessfulness is assigned, "Ye ask amiss." Those that prayed were none of the best, the manner of their asking was bad; and so was their end and design. They were petitioners to God, that they might have wherewithal to serve their lusts and pleasures.

The **DOCTRINE** which I raise from the words is this: *Although we ask, we shall not receive, if our asking is amiss.* It is to be feared that many, if not most prayers miscarry. The Lord has indeed styled himself as a hearer of prayer; but many supplicants are such, and their supplications so sorry, that they do not regard what they do, and it is no wonder that God has no regard to their heartless and formal devotion. Fervent prayer has a promise of obedience, but hypocritical services have a threatening, that God's eye shall be hidden, and his ear will be deaf to them. "When you spread forth your hands, I will hide mine eyes from you; yea, when you make many prayers I will not hear," (Isaiah 1:15). We read that cries sent to heaven, brought down no help from there, the people cried amiss, "They cried but their was none to save; even to the Lord, but he answered them not," (Psalm 18:41).

In the handling of this doctrine, I *shall*:

First, show you when we may be said to ask amiss.

Second, give you the reasons why when we ask amiss, we shall not receive.

Last, conclude with the application.

HOW CHRISTIANS ASK AMISS IN PRAYER

In the first place I am to show you when we may be said to ask amiss. But before I insist on this, I must premise one thing of mighty importance and concernment to be taken notice of. That there is no asking of the best saint in the world, but there is something amiss about it. Who can say that his heart is made quite clean? Or that his duties have no faults at all in them? The apostle himself (and the church could never show man a better) acknowledges, "I find them a law, that when I would do good, evil is present with me," (Romans 7:21). When the lusts of the spirit and its desires are never so strong and holy, there are some lusts of the flesh that are quite contrary; so that believers themselves cannot do the things that they would, nor so well as they wish. The most spiritual sacrifices that the most spiritual man can offer up to God, could not be accepted on their own account, but "became acceptable through Jesus Christ," (1 Peter 2:5).

So that all asking amiss shall not hinder the receiving of what we ask at the hand of God; if our asking amiss is a matter of our trouble, and we are deeply humbled because our duties are no better performed; if we take pains with our hearts, that we may pray with greater intention and fervency, and implore the Spirit's aid, that both for matter and manner, we may pray more according to the will of God. And if after all we look to Jesus, our merciful and faithful High Priest, in things pertaining to God, that the sins of our holy things may be pardoned, and the imperfections of our best duties may be covered by his righteousness.

I now come to show when we may be said to ask amiss in the sense of the text; when we may be said to pray so, that all our prayers are lost; and we ourselves shall be lost too, notwithstanding all our prayers.

We ask amiss, when those things are lacking in our prayers that might make them acceptable. And we ask amiss, when those things accompany our prayers, that will certainly render them abominable.

In the first place, we ask amiss when those things are lacking in our prayers that might make them acceptable. And several things are necessarily requisite to the acceptance of them.

1. We ask amiss when prayer is without contrition and brokenness of heart; because God whom we pray to, has been offended by sin. When offenders make their addresses to the glorious and highest majesty, without any trouble that they have offended him; this impudence and hard-heartedness of theirs makes him to be more highly offended at them. He must necessarily be the more displeased, because they are so little displeased themselves at their misdoings. He looks with compassion and favor to the contrite and lowly; but "the

proud he knows afar off," (Psalm 138:6). He knows them too well to admit them to any fellowship with himself; and they are too full of enmity to desire it. The psalmist tells us, that the "Lord is nigh to them who are of a broken heart, and saveth such as be of a contrite spirit," (Psalm 34:18). He is near to hear them and to work that salvation which they desire and need; but those who have no sense of sin, that do not look on it as a matter of shame, as a grounds of grief, as worthy of extreme hatred; their stupidity, which they are rather glad of, than wish to be rid of; is such a provocation, that prayer cannot be accepted. The cries of the hard-hearted do not move God's bowels of mercy and compassion.

2. We ask amiss when we do not ask in faith. "But let him ask in faith nothing wavering, for he that wavereth is like a wave of the sea driven with the wind and tossed; for let not that man think that he shall receive anything of the Lord," (James 1:6-7). It is most evident from this Scripture that the success of prayer depends on the acting of faith in the heart; there will be no audience from heaven. Now this praying in faith comprehends a great deal in it. He that prays must be in the faith; he must believe the certainty of the Word of God; the truth of the Gospel of Christ. Those that call themselves deists and worship God, if they refuse to make use of Christ's mediation; their prayers are despised, and they shall perish in their iniquities. "If ye believe not that I am He, ye shall die in

your sins," (John 8:24). He that prays in faith is persuaded in some measure of God's ability and readiness in Christ to perform those promises he has made; and that to him in particular; if he truly repents of sin, and relies on the Lord Jesus for the blessings which are promised.

Here it may be asked, whether assurance is not necessary for praying in faith? I answer: the more there is of a well-grounded assurance in him that prays, prayer will have the richer return. He that knows God as his Father, and does not doubt that what he asks shall be given to him much more readily than earthly parents will give good things to their asking children. That kind of confidence shall not make the believer ashamed. "And this is the confidence that we have in him, that if we ask anything according to his will, he hears us; and if we know that he hears us we know that we have the petitions we desired of him. Yet this must be added, that if we trust in God and rely on him through his dear Son, to perform his promise and to make us qualified and fit for that mercy and grace which he has promised; and we desire to partake of, though we may distrust ourselves; yet trusting in God to work all in us, as well as for us, we really pray in faith, though not in full assurance.

3. We ask amiss if our asking is without reverence and godly fear. If there is no awful sense of the greatness of God with whom we have to do; nor of the greatness of our wants,

which only he can supply, and which if they are supplied, we must necessarily be miserable forever. A constant allowed slightness of spirit in our supplications will quite spoil them. How can we in reason hope that the Lord should graciously mind what we do, when we do not seriously mind what we are doing ourselves? If Christians are to feed themselves in fear, if they are to be in the fear of the Lord all the day long, whatever they are doing, certainly this holy fear should be in great exercise, in all their acts of worship. If you do not mind the God you pray to, nor how you serve him, nor how you succeed in the service you perform, but rest in a bare external performance; Alas! Time is unprofitably wasted, and guilt is increased by such heartless unlawful worship.

It was the psalmist's resolution when he came into the house of God, to join in hope in the mercy of the Lord, and a reverence of his majesty together; "As for me I will come into thy house in the multitude of thy mercy; and in thy fear will I worship towards thy holy temple," (Psalm 5:7). And such an awe and fear was not only under the old testament, but it is also required under the new; no, it is an effect and fruit of the grace of Christ's kingdom, "Wherefore we receiving a kingdom that cannot be moved, let us have grace by which we may serve God acceptably with reverence and Godly fear; for our God is a consuming fire," (Hebrews 12:28-29). God is terrible out of his holy place; it is the height of madness to kindle the fire of his jealousy against us, by our careless services; since he is so infinitely above us, and stronger than we.

4. We ask amiss when we do not use the prevailing Name of Jesus Christ, the Mediator. The sons of men who are guilty and defiled can never come to a righteous and holy God; nor have any communion with him but through a Mediator; and though there are many that are called Mediators, yet to the true Christian church, there is only one God, so only "one Mediator between God and men, the man Christ Jesus who gave himself a ransom for all," (1 Timothy 2:5-6). This Mediator's blood was shed a great while ago on earth, but it cries in heaven to this hour, and it cries for those very blessings for which believers pray. This merciful and faithful High Priest is at the right hand of God; and there he is by his satisfaction and intercession to make reconciliation for sin, and "to procure grace and succor for us against temptations," (Hebrews 2:17-18). The blood of Christ cries to God, that what has been purchased by it may be bestowed on those that believe in him; now all things are purchased, and to whom Christ is given, nothing will be denied, "He that spared not his own Son, but delivered him up for us all; how shall he not with him also freely give us all things!" (Romans 8:32).

But those who do not use this Name of Jesus, can never speedily speak to God, "for there is no other name under heaven given among men by which we can be saved," (Acts 4:12). And those that join other mediators, as saints and angels in heaven, with him, dishonor him; and how is their confidence drawn off from him as if he were not a sufficient advocate! Nothing can be done aright "either in word or in deed, but in the Name of the Lord Jesus," (Colossians 3:17).

5. We ask amiss when spiritual blessings are undervalued and postponed. When they are either not at all, or not chiefly desired. A carnal man may cry to God for worldly blessings. These are pleasing to his worldly heart; and having received them, he abuses them to the dishonor of Him that bestows them; and turns them into weapons of rebellion against him. We read of assemblies that cried to God, but God himself they did not seek, but something from him, which they made a very bad and impious use of: "They assemble themselves for corn and wine, and they rebel against me," (Hosea 7:14).

Christians that are only so in name discover the unsoundness of their hearts by the channel in which the stream of their desires run. They desire and pray for health, ease, peace, liberty, plenty, for length of days, and all prosperous; and when any of these kind of mercies are wanting, they have a very quick sense of that lack, and their desires are more earnest. The continuance of earthly enjoyments is begged; and especially if any of them are taken away, that they may be restored.

But though they desire much at God's hand, yet communion with him is not valued. Promises are not looked at as precious, by which they might be made partakers of the divine nature, a new heart, the sanctifying Spirit and plenteous redemption from all iniquity. These are the blessings that are most true and desirable, yet carnal hearts do not desire them, but choose rather to be without them.

I grant that our Lord instructed his disciples to pray for daily bread; so that temporal mercies in their place, (which I am sure should not be the chief and highest) may be desired; but it is much to be observed, that there is in the Lord's prayer only one petition for daily bread, but several petitions of another kind; that God's Name might be hallowed and glorified; that his kingdom might come with power into our own and other's hearts; and that we might do the will of God on earth as it is in heaven; that our trespasses might be forgiven; and that the grace of God may be sufficient for us to preserve us from the tempter's power. He asks rightly who from his heart can put up every petition in the Lord's prayer; but certainly they ask very much amiss, who heartily desire nothing but daily bread; to which, the good things of this present world; and fear of wrath in the other world makes them beg that their trespasses may be forgiven; but yet they will venture the missing of a pardon, rather than consent that no iniquity should have the dominion over them.

6. We ask amiss, when we do not ask by the Spirit's aid. Scoffers prate against and deride praying by the Spirit. But I am sure that none can speed in their requests, unless He instructs their ignorance and helps their infirmities. As he teaches saints to profit; so he teaches them how to pray. If our supplications are only the fruit of our natural parts, our common gifts, our invention and notional knowledge, and the labor of our lips, they will not be accepted. As there is an absolute necessity of Christ's intercession for us in heaven; so there is a necessity of the Spirit's interceding on earth.

But how does the Spirit intercede? I answer: He excites and stirs up gracious and holy desires in the saints; he shows them what petitions agree with divine promises; and what it is that is agreeable to the will of God. The truth is, right prayer is τὸ φρόνημα τοῦ πνεύματος, the mind of the Spirit. "And he that searcheth the heart, knoweth what is the mind of the spirit; because he maketh intercession for the saints according to the will of God," (Romans 8:27). And how can he choose but to pray well, who speaks to God the mind of God's own Spirit; and also has Christ to be his advocate! But without the illumination and assistance of the Holy Ghost, none know what to pray for as they ought; therefore their requests will be the venting of their own minds, their own wills, the corrupt inclinations, passions , and affections of their own hearts; and how can God be pleased with them?

7. We ask amiss when we do not make the Lord himself our highest end in our prayers. The soul of him that prays should "follow hard after God," (Psalm 63:8). Only He who is the Father of immortal spirits can be their satisfaction and their rest. But if the Lord is followed after, not that he may give himself but some other enjoyment; that enjoyment is preferred before him; and his jealous eye cannot help but take notice of it with great displeasure. Many in sickness seek the Lord, and pour out a prayer before him; but it is only that health may be restored; that is their design and end; and if that is recovered, they seek no further, they look no higher; the glory of God is not in their eye, nor their own sanctification; and that affliction may yield the peaceable fruits of righteousness. Many pray that they may prosper in the world; not that by prosperity they may be lead to God, but God is sought out for the sake of prosperity; and if that is obtained and continued, they are very well satisfied, though they are strangers to God, and to fellowship with him.

If the all-sufficient God is not our end in prayer, and we only make use of him that we may enjoy something else, prayer is only a discovery of how much we slight him, for we address to him for mere trifles comparatively, whereas he would have us to seek himself, his righteousness, and his kingdom.

So you can see when those things are lacking in prayers that might make them acceptable.

ABOMINABLE PRAYERS

In the second place, we ask amiss when our prayers are accompanied by those things that will certainly make them abominable.

I shall mention several abominable concomitants of *prayer*:

1. Our asking is amiss, if notwithstanding our praying and professing, we allow ourselves in the unfruitful works of darkness. To cry to God, and talk of fellowship with him, and yet to walk in darkness; in ways that are false, and which he hates; this is to show ourselves to be liars, "and we do not the truth," (1 John 11:6). We are far from calling on God in truth, neither shall we find him to be near to us in anything which we call on him for. Those that draw near to God must lift up holy hands to him; "I will therefore that men pray everywhere, lifting up holy hands," (1 Timothy 2:8). How good the words are which the tongue speaks; how fluent and excellent the expressions are in prayer. God is very angry to hear them, as long as he sees that evil works are the ordinary practice.

Allowed iniquity will render prayer ineffectual; for the worker of iniquity speaks like a servant, and says, "Lord, Lord;" but he acts like an enemy, and according to his works, he shall be dealt with.

We read if many that performed holy duties and were also very confident of their own acceptance; they concluded that their prayers entered into heaven, and had no doubt that they would have an abundant entrance at last. They knock at the door, and say, "Lord, Lord, open to us!" But to their eternal consternation and sorrow, they are thrust away and excluded with the sentence, "I know you not whence you are; depart from me all ye workers of iniquity," (Luke 13:27). Christ never knew them to do as they should; they never prayed as they ought; they often came into his presence, but always brought their sins along with them, and they carried them away again. The Lord's work must necessarily be done to no purpose, as long as they remained workers of iniquity.

2. Our asking is amiss, though our lives are unspotted, if we regard iniquity in our hearts; "If I regard iniquity in my heart, the Lord will not hear my prayer," (Psalm 66:18). Though our hands are restrained from evil works, and our feet refrain from evil ways, yet if sin reigns in our hearts, and we love and delight in it, shall God not search this out? "For he knoweth the secrets of the heart," (Psalm 44:21). Regarding iniquity in the heart implies conniving at it; endeavoring to

hide and secure it by excuses; taking such pleasure in heart-wickedness, as to resolve by no means to part with it. And a heart of this ill inclination, how estranged from God it must be! And though his hand is not shortened, nor his ear heavy, yet regarded "iniquity will separate between the soul and the Lord, and he will hide away his face, and refuse to hear, (Jeremiah 59:1-2).

The wicked man must forsake his evil way and his thoughts; his feet and his heart must turn together from all sin to God. Then if he seeks the Lord, he will find him near, and he is "most ready to be found," (Isaiah 55:6-7). But if sin has the heart at its command, the heart shall not be permitted to be in any duty; and heartless duties are done very much amiss. Therefore when the psalmist prayed for mercy, he prayed for a clean heart and a right spirit at the same time. "Create in me a clean heart, O God, and renew a right spirit within me," (Psalm 51:10). He knew very well if he did not have such a heart, such a spirit, he should not be accepted of God. "My son," says God, "give thy heart to me:" If regard to sin hinders the heart from being given to God, all that is offered besides will be offered amiss, and be contemptible in his eyes.

3. Our asking is amiss when this world, notwithstanding our duties, has been made our idol by our loving and serving it. A man that is covetous and earthly-minded, never put up a right prayer to God in his life; and

until the iniquity of his covetousness is subdued, he never will. The same may be affirmed concerning those who are so much taken with worldly pleasure, and applause, and honor from men. Those who love any earthly enjoyment, and creature whatever, more than God; this spiritually adulterous and idolatrous love will make all their duties and themselves too, hateful to that Lord whom they pretend to worship.

There are two masters spoken of in Scripture, and they are contrary one to another; so that no man can serve them both, "Ye cannot," says our Lord, "serve God and mammon," (Matthew 6:24). If mammon has your hearts, God does not have them; and how can you expect to see the Lord's face if your hearts are not with him? The lover of the world is the world's idolater; and this is the language that his heart speaks to the world when it is worshipped, "How good O mammon, and how great and how desirable are thou in my eyes! They that speak to thy disparagement, do either dissemble a disesteem of thee; or are ignorant of thy worth and excellence. Thy treasures are the truest riches which are most worthy to be coveted after! Thy delights are of all the sweetest, and most suitable to the sons of men! They who are wise to get and keep thee, are the wisest men indeed. You, O Mammon are my confidence in dangers! My expectation of supplies is from you. You are the height of my desires; the top of my ambition; the chief end which I propose to myself in all my labors. As your enjoyments are diminished or augmented, so does my joy and comfort ebb or flow. Life is desirable for thy sake; and I think of death with horror, because it will part between you and me forever.

Those whose hearts speak of the world after this manner; whatever they say to God, is most impious hypocrisy; and he cannot but be very much incensed and displeased to behold mammon in such high esteem; and himself and service slighted and condemned.

4. Our asking is amiss when we take no care to have our hearts emptied of wrath, and our unruly passions. If we are sinfully angry with others, God is justly angry with us. As the wrath of man does not work the righteousness of God, so it is an ill comparison of the duties which are performed to him. Our Lord Jesus, vindicating the law from the cursed and corrupt glosses of the scribes and Pharisees, and showing how extensive it is; and reaches the very soul and conscience. It tells us plainly, that as looking on a woman, to lust after her, is committing adultery in the heart; so being angry without a cause is a heart murder. When anger unreasonably prevails, you have reason to cry out, "Deliver me from blood-guiltiness O God!"

When we lift up our hands to God, there must not be doubting or wrath in our hearts, (1 Timothy 2:8). The fire of passion and fury is strange fire; it is indeed wildfire; it is dangerous to come with it before the Lord. That caution is highly needful, "Let all bitterness, and wrath, and clamor, and evil speaking, be put away from you, with all kind of malice; and be ye kind one to another, tender-hearted; forgiving one another, even as God for Christ's sake hath forgiven you," (Ephesians 4:31-32). After our Lord had given his disciples that admirable excellent "pattern of prayer," (Matthew 6:9) to show how a wrathful and implacable temper of spirit would hinder prayer's success; he signifies that if they would not forgive their brethren, they themselves should not be forgiven. "For if ye forgive men their trespasses, your heavenly Father will also forgive you; but if ye forgive not men their trespasses, neither will your Father forgive your trespasses," (Matthew 6:14-15).

5. Our asking is amiss when the matter of our prayers is unlawful, and the end and design is sinful. Those petitions must necessarily be very abominable, when men beg a blessing from heaven on those wicked courses which lead directly to hell; and that their unrighteous ways may prove prosperous; and they may bring their wicked devices to pass. I have heard a relation of some pirates who used to pray daily for a good booty; though all that they received was gotten so unjustly and in a bad manner.

The poet presented these petitions to *heaven:*

Da mihi fallere, da justum sanctumq; viderit!

Noctem peccatis, & fraudibus objice nubem!

He begged that he might be successful in his cheats and knavery; and that he might still seem to be just and holy; and that all his frauds and wickedness might be hidden in a cloud and darkness from those whom he dealt with. It is to be feared that these are the secret wishes of too many professors of religion; and if they are hearty in anything, it is in desires of this nature. And as prayer is unlawful if the matter of it is abominable; so also, though the matter is innocent, if the end and design are evil. Thus those in the text asked amiss; what they obtained by prayer, they intended to consume it on their lusts; were progging for their lusts, even when they were at the throne of grace. The Lord had some service from them, that thereby they might obtain something from his hand that they might make the more plenteous provision for the flesh, to fulfill its lusts.

Many will pray for fruitful seasons, for a thriving trade, for plenty of good and raiment, and an abundance of worldly comforts; but in the all this they seek themselves, they design the pleasing of themselves, the gratifying of their appetites and senses; and such a brutish and sensual felicity is taken up with. God, the giver of all to them, they "care not how they displease and despise." They do not mind the enjoyment of him, but only outward enjoyments from him. Thus the rich man desired fruitful fields, and full barns; and his end was that he might take his ease, eat, drink, and be merry; and in the meantime, the securing of his soul, and becoming rich towards God, was most wickedly, wretchedly, and sottishly neglected, (Luke 12:19-21).

6. Our asking is amiss when we stop our ears against the cries of our poor distressed brethren; "Whoso stoppeth his ears at the cry of the poor, he also shall cry himself, but shall not be heard," (Proverbs 21:13): He may be brought into low circumstances, and reduced to great poverty, and may then meet with deaf ears, shut hands, and hard hearts; being unpittied in his distress, and reap the just fruit of his own unmercifulness. But it is certain that God will not regard the cry of the unmerciful man. It is very provoking to have the heart hardened against God, and from his fear; and it is likewise a very great provocation to have a heart hardened against those who are in distress, to have no bowels stirring towards them in their misery. Dreadful is that threatening, "He shall have judgment without mercy who hath shewed no mercy," (James 2:13).

It is a certain truth, those that are merciful to men have a promise of mercy from God; "Blessed are the merciful, for they shall obtain mercy," (Matthew 5:7). Those that rightly consider the poor; who put their own souls in their soul's stead; and sympathize with them in their poverty and sufferings, and are ready to their power to show mercy to them; such may cry with confidence to be delivered, when they are in trouble. For the Lord has promised to preserve them, to keep them alive, and they shall be blessed on earth. Divine care of them shall be tender; the Lord will vouchsafe a presence that shall be most supporting and refreshing to them; "The Lord will strengthen him on the bed of languishing; thou wilt make all his bed in his sickness," (Psalm 41:3).

But on the contrary, hard-heartedness to our poor brethren is laid down in Scripture as one of the blackest and deadliest marks of those who are hateful to God; and who shall have no help from him; "But whoso hath this world's goods, and seeth his brother have need, and shutteth up his bowels of compassion from him; how dwelleth the love of God in him?" (1 John 3:17).

7. Our asking is amiss when we deaden our ears to the law, and to the word of God. The Lord speaks to us by the ministry of his word; we speak to him by prayer. We must hearken to God, that God may hearken to us. Our deafness and disobedience to his voice is threatened with his deafness to our cries; in our greatest distress and anguish; nay so far will he be from pitying that he will mock us in our misery; "Because I have called, and ye refused; I have stretched out my hand, and no man regarded; But ye have set at nought all my

counsel, and would have none of my reproof: I also will laugh at your calamity; I will mock when your fear cometh; when your fear cometh as desolation, and your destruction cometh as a whirlwind; when distress and anguish cometh upon you. Then shall they call upon me, but I will not answer; they shall seek me early, but they shall not find me," (Proverbs 1:24-28). Hear this, you church-sleepers; consider how dangerous it is for man to not mind when God vouchsafes to speak to him! Hear this, all whose hearts go after the world, even while you are in God's sanctuary. How can you in reason expect that the Lord's ear should be open to you, considering how yours are fast shut against him; when he gives you the most needful warnings to flee from the most dreadful wrath and vengeance! When he makes you the greatest offers that can be made, of no less than special grace, and everlasting life and glory! When he gives you commandments, none of which are grievous, but all of them holy, just and good!

Deafness to the Word of God will make all asking to be amiss. God will disregard that man's prayer, who has no regard to his Word. "Whoso turneth away his ear from hearing the law, even his prayer shall be an abomination," (Proverbs 28:9). And we find this verified, "They stopped their ears, they made their hearts like an adamant stone, lest they should hear the law, and the words which the Lord of hosts hath sent in his Spirit by the former prophets; therefore came there a great wrath from the Lord of hosts. Therefore it is come to pass, that as he cried and they would not hear, so they cried and I would not hear, saith the Lord of hosts," (Zachariah 7:12-13).

So I have shown you when we may be said to ask amiss.

WHY WE ASK AMISS

In the second place, I am to give you the reasons why when we ask amiss, we shall not receive; and in so plain and evident a matter. I need to do little more than to name them.

1. There is no promise of God made to such as those who ask amiss. He promises indeed to be found of such as those who seek him in his own way, with their whole heart; but no promise is made to lip labor; when the heart is not right with God, but removed far from him, no, worship in this case, is pronounced vain, (Matthew 15:8-9).

2. Asking amiss is not seconded by the intercession of Christ, the only prevailing Advocate with the Father. His blood does not speak for those who are not poor in spirit, nor sensible of their own wants. As he "came not to call the righteous, but sinners to repentance," (Matthew 9:13), so with his intercession he backs the prayers, not of those who trust in their own righteousness, or are unsensible of their

iniquities; but of those that are convinced of sin, and look to Him both as a Mediator and Physician, that they may be pardoned and healed.

3. This asking amiss is provoking of God to his very face. It is an affronting of him, as if he has neither eyes, nor ears to observe, nor power in his hand to avenge himself on those that offend him. We read of some that separated themselves from God; and set up their idols in their hearts; and put the stumbling blocks of their iniquity before their face, and yet came to seek and inquire of God. Now, says the Lord, I will answer such men by myself; and I will set my face against them, and will make every one of them a "sign and a proverb; and I will cut them off from the midst of my people; and ye shall know that I am the Lord," (Ezekiel 14:7-8).

I now come to the application of the doctrine; and the inferences which may be drawn from it are these *two*:

1. If those that ask amiss do not receive, learn from hence the reason why so many prayers are made that are not answered. Is the Lord's hand shortened or his ears heavy or his bowels less tender than they were? It would be the height of foolishness to charge and blame him, for God is most willing to hear and give; but thousands that pray ask amiss, and do not care to ask better; and so are utterly unfit and unprepared to receive.

We have prayed for peace, but the sword of war will not rest and be quiet; it is not put up into the sheath to this day; it costs much blood, much treasure, and is likely to be expensive of much more. We have prayed for victory, yet enemies are in their *ruff and power*; how are the French daily enriched with English spoils! We have prayed for the reviving and increase of trade, but poverty prevails both in the city and country, like and armed man: And the reason why is because there is so much amiss in them.

What kind of persons are the most that ask! How little humility, faith, sincerity, fervency in the manner of asking! People must alter for the better, hearts being purified, ways and doings thoroughly amended; prayers also must alter for the better; or else God will still be angry at them, and deaf to them: we must "cease to do evil, learn to do well," (Isaiah 1:16-17). And if once we are washed and made clean, and put away the evil of our doings from before God's eyes; what glorious and gracious returns would prayer have. That Lord whom we pray to would "soon subdue our enemies, and turn his hand against our adversaries!" (Psalm 81:14) and make an alteration for the better in the whole state of our affairs!

2. Learn from hence how little reason they have to expect that they shall receive, who do not ask at all. Those that live without prayer, cast off the fear of God and live without him in the world. We read of some that speak this

impious language, "What is the Almighty that we should serve him? and what profit should we have if we pray to him," (Job 21:15). Such have departed very far from God, and are utterly estranged from him; they are advanced a great way in the road to ruin; and are on the very brink of the bottomless pit; and whatever they have, comes to them big with the curse of God; and proves a snare and a stumbling block; so that they fall more into sin and deeper into destruction and perdition.

How many prayerless houses are there in London to this day, and that notwithstanding the loud calls of late from me, to call on God! These houses are the shame of London, and how prejudicial to the city! Many masters of families spend so much time in clubs, in ale houses, coffee houses, and taverns; that none can be allowed for family duties. And the heads of families, so profanely neglecting religion, all under their care may be the more strongly induced to follow their wicked and pernicious example. So families are nurseries for sin, Satan, and mammon; and parents and masters, as if they were factors for hell, bring up their children and servants in gross ignorance and great contempt of God and godliness.

It can never be sufficiently bewailed that God is so forgotten in days without number; and that the worship and homage which is due to him, is denied him! But do not let men deceive themselves, God will not be mocked. Those that do not think it is worth their time to pray for blessings shall go without them; and those that will not ask for the taking away of sin and wrath, have both abiding on them. The apostle charges us to "pray always with all prayers," (Ephesians 6:18) and so considering our mighty enemies, our great danger; all is little enough for our security. But those who instead of praying with all prayer, refuse to pray at all; they are fearless of their spiritual adversaries; and so are more under their power. In their practice they deny that God is worthy to be worshipped, and in effect they say, "It is vain to hope for any good from him; or to fear any evil at his hands." The best things of all will such go without, and endless evils are at the door.

BEING SURE TO RECEIVE WHAT YOU ASK FOR

Use 2 shall be of direction, how you may ask rightly and be sure to receive what you ask for.

1. That you may ask rightly, look upward that your hearts may be prepared for this duty of prayer. "The preparation of the heart in man is of the Lord," (Proverbs 16:1). An unprepared heart will make very sorry work at the throne of grace; the unpreparedness will cry more against it, than the tongue can speak for it. This is the divine method; when the Lord intends to give, he prepares and fits the soul to receive; "Thou wilt prepare their heart, thou wilt cause thine ear to

hear," (Psalm 10:17). When you are to engage in prayer, remember it is a work above your strength; call in therefore a strength beyond your own.

Look to the Lord that you may be able to look to him rightly. Cry that you may be helped to cry as you should. It is He alone that can call your hearts off from other businesses, that you may intend prayer. It is he alone that can fix your thoughts on himself, and give a rebuke to Satan, who stands at your right hand to resist you; and He alone can effectually check that evil which is present with you when you desire to do that which is good. When you are about to pray, be sure to lift up your souls to God, that they may be made fit for communion with him, and communications of grace from him.

2. I commend to you the poverty of spirit. Be sensible of your manifold wants, and of your worthlessness as you cannot supply your own needs; so you are unworthy to have them supplied, or you are wretched forever, and they must be supplied quickly, or it will be too late to have them supplied at all. If you do not now obtain mercy and saving grace, glory will be missed of. The deeper your apprehension is, how poor and needy you are, the stronger and more earnest your cries will be: "But I am poor and needy, make haste to help me O God; thou art my help and my deliverer, O Lord make no tarrying," (Psalm 70:5). The kingdom is promised to the poor in spirit, "Blessed are the poor in spirit for theirs is the

kingdom of heaven," (Matthew 5:3); and they shall be supplied with all things by the way until they are brought safely there; "For all those things hath my hand made, and all those things have been saith the Lord; but to this man will I look, that is poor and of a contrite spirit, and trembleth at my word," (Isaiah 66:2).

3. That you may ask rightly, you must be upright yourselves, and sincere before God. Unfeignedly consent to be thoroughly searched to have all sin discovered; and to be sanctified throughout the body, in soul and spirit. Willingly cover no transgression, neither hide your eyes from any command, or commanded duty. Sincerely desire to know the will of God, and grace and strength from him to do it being made known to you. Acknowledge God in all your ways; and look on it as your wisdom to follow his guidance; and often open your hearts to him, that he may both search and cleanse them. Prayers that come from an upright heart, meet with an open ear; "The sacrifice of the wicked is an abomination to the Lord, but the prayer of the upright is his delight," (Proverbs 15:8). "I know also O my God that thou tryest the heart, and hast pleasure in uprightness," (1 Chronicles 29:17). What gracious answer upright ones have when they pray to God! His eye, his ear, his hand, his heart, are all open to them! He loves them; he loves to hear and help them; and to make them exceedingly glad with his countenance. "For the righteous

Lord loveth righteousness, his countenance doth behold the upright.

4. Let Jesus the Mediator be your hope and confidence in all your supplications. Be sure to worship God in the Spirit, with your own spirits, and by the help of His; but when you have done so, rejoice in Christ Jesus, as the foundation of your hope and expectation, and "have no confidence in the flesh," (Philippians 3:3). Though you are never so fervent and enlarged in prayer, and the duty seems to be very spiritually performed; if your dependence is not on the Advocate with the Father, but the duty itself is rested on for acceptance, you are to be charged with carnal confidence, "Whatever you do in word or in deed, do all in the name of the Lord Jesus," (Colossians 3:17). You are strangers to the right and successful, and acceptable way of praying, unless you know that "Christ is given to be Head over all things to the church; and he fills all in all," (Ephesians 1:22-23). What an assuring assertion our Lord gives us! "Verily, verily, I say unto you, whatsoever ye shall ask the Father in my name, he will give it you. Thus ask and ye shall receive, that your joy may be full," (John 16:23-24).

5. In prayer, be most fervent for those blessings that are most valuable. Our Lord would not have us to be so earnest in seeking earthly things: These, heathens are taken with; but Christians should look on, as below them. What we

need of things of this nature, our Heavenly Father knows better than we. But, says Christ, "Seek ye first the kingdom of God and the righteousness thereof, and all things shall be added to you," (Matthew 6:22). Your desire should be strongest after the blessings of that kingdom; after a justifying righteousness; after inherent grace and holiness; together with peace of conscience and joy in the Holy Ghost; and at last an incorruptible inheritance. Value and pray hard for these and they are your own; and temporal blessings shall be flung in over and above. If you desire in the first and chief place to have grace and glory, that God whom you seek will withhold no other think from you, which he knows to be indeed good for you, (Psalm 84:11).

6. That you may ask rightly, let there be more of charity and of a public spirit in your supplications. If all things are to be done with charity, (1 Corinthians 16:14) the duty of prayer cannot be well done without it. A root of bitterness in your spirits against your brethren, will provoke the God of love and peace to frown on you, when you come before him; and it will be very apt to distract your thoughts and to put your hearts quite out of a praying frame. Mind the apostle's admonition, "Put on therefore (as the elect of God, holy and beloved) bowels of mercies, kindness, humbleness of mind, meekness, long-suffering; forbearing one another, and forgiving one another, if any man has a quarrel against and as

Christ forgave you, so also do ye," (Colossians 3:12). Saints are to love their enemies and persecutors; how inexcusable are they if they do not love one another!

All saints should be on the heart of every saint. Every member should be concerned for the whole body of Christ on earth. He is a genuine son of Zion, and likely to prevail both for the church and for himself too, whose resolution is such as we find: "For Zion's sake will I not hold my peace, and for Jerusalem's sake I will not rest, until the righteousness thereof goes forth as brightness, and the salvation thereof as a lamp that burneth," (Isaiah 62:1).

7. That you may ask rightly, promise praise if you do it speedily, and let practice agree with prayer. When David begged for mercy and the healing of his backslidings, as he offered up the sacrifice of a broken heart, so he promised to offer up to God the sacrifice of thanksgiving: "O Lord, thou my lips, and my mouth shall shew forth thy praise: and my tongue shall sing aloud of thy righteousness." The Church begs for help in their low estate, and they promise gratitude: "So we that are thy people and sheep of thy pasture, will give thee thanks forever: we will shew forth thy praise to all generations," (Psalm 79:13).

And after you have been praying, look to your practice. He that lives ill can never pray well. The hands of Esau do not agree at all with the voice of Jacob. The more you live your prayers, the more God will regard them. "Whatsoever we ask we receive of him, because we keep his commandments, and do those things that are pleasing in his sight."

FINIS

www.ingramcontent.com/pod-product-compliance
Lightning Source LLC
Chambersburg PA
CBHW032002080426
42735CB00007B/480